The Aquarian Sun

**Bernard Fitzwalter** has been interested in astology since he was about six, when he played King Herod's astrologer in his primary school nativity play. For the past six years he has been teaching astrology for the Marylebone-Paddington Institute, and for seven years he has had a regular column in OVER 21 magazine. In 1984 he appeared in the first series of Anglia Television's *Zodiac Game*, which prompted the *Daily Mirror* to say that he was 'enough to give astrology a good name'.

# AQUARIAN SUN SIGN GUIDES

# AQUARIUS

## 20 JANUARY - 19 FEBRUARY

### Bernard Fitzwalter

*Cover illustration by Steinar Lund*
*Cover typography by Steven Lee*

THE AQUARIAN PRESS
Wellingborough, Northamptonshire

First published 1987

© BERNARD FITZWALTER 1987

British Library Cataloguing in Publication Data

Fitzwalter, Bernard
Aquarius.—(The Aquarian sun sign guides)
1. Zodiac
1. Title
133.5'4    BF1728.A2

ISBN 0-85030-574-8

*The Aquarian Press is part of the
Thorsons Publishing Group*

Printed and bound in Great Britain

# Contents

## PART 4: AQUARIUS TRIVIA

# Introduction

This book has been written to help you find out a little about astrology and a lot about yourself. It explains, for the first time, the motives and aims that guide your actions and make you do things the way you do; what it does not do is give you a list of 'typical Aquarius' things to see if you recognize any of them. You are not likely to be typical anything: you are unique. What you *do* have in common with others who have birthdays at about the same time as you is a way of using your energy, a way of thinking, a set of motives and beliefs which seem to make sense to you, and which other people, those of the other eleven signs, obviously do not have. This book shows you those motives and beliefs, and shows you how they fit in with those of the other eleven signs. The zodiac is like a jigsaw: all the pieces have to be there for the whole picture to emerge.

This book also sets out to answer some very simple questions which are often asked but seldom answered. Questions like 'Why does the zodiac have twelve signs?' and 'What does being an Aquarius actually mean?' as well as 'Why are Aquarians supposed to be cool and aloof? Why can't they be passionate instead?' and 'Why don't all the people of the same star sign look the same?'

The reason that these questions are seldom answered is because all too many astrologers don't know the rudiments of astrological theory, and what they do know they don't tell, because they think it is too difficult for the man in the street to understand. This is obvious nonsense: astrology was devised for and by people who did not normally read or write as much as we do, nor did they all have PhDs or the equivalent. The man in the street is quite capable of understanding anything provided that it is shown simply and clearly, from first principles upwards, and provided he has sufficient interest. Buying this book is evidence enough of your interest, and I hope that the explanations are simple enough and clear enough for you. If they are not, it is my fault, and not that of astrology.

## How to Use this Book

The book is in four parts. It is best to read them in sequence, but if you have neither time nor patience, then they each work individually. Part 2 does not assume that you have read Part 1, though it helps. Part 3 makes a lot more sense if you have already read Parts 1 and 2, but it isn't mandatory. Part 4, although just as astrologically deep as the other three, is definitely intended as light relief to bring you back to real life gently after some of the more thought-provoking stuff.

The first part of the book deals with the theory behind the zodiac; it sets out the principles of astrology and enables you to see why Aquarius is assigned the qualities it has, how the ruling planet system works, and what all the other signs are like in terms of motivation, so you can compare them to your own. There is a short and effective method given for assessing the aims and motives of other people. When you read Part 3 you will need to know a bit about the other signs, as you will be finding out that you have more to you than just the Aquarius part you knew about.

The second part describes the essential Aquarius. It shows you how there are different sorts of Aquarians according to where your birthday falls in the month, and shows how Aquarian energy is used differently in the Aquarius as a child, adult, and parent.

Since you spend the greatest part of your life in dealing with other individuals, the way Aquarius deals with relationships is treated in some detail. This is the largest part of the book.

The third part shows you a different kind of zodiac, and enables you to go into your own life in much greater detail. It isn't complicated, but you do need to think. It crosses the border between the kind of astrology you get in the magazines, and the sort of thing a real astrologer does. There's no reason why you can't do it yourself because, after all, you know yourself best.

The fourth part shows you the surface of being an Aquarius, and how that zodiacal energy comes out in your clothes, your home, even your favourite food. The final item of this part actually explains the mechanics of being lucky, which you probably thought was impossible.

I hope that when you finish reading you will have a clearer view of yourself, and maybe like yourself a little more. Don't throw the book away; read it again in a few months' time—you will be surprised at what new thoughts about yourself it prompts you to form!

## A Final Note

Throughout this book, the pronouns 'he', 'him', and 'his' have been used to describe both male and female. Everything which applies to a male Aquarian applies to a female Aquarian as well. There are two reasons why I have not bothered to make the distinction: firstly, to avoid long-windedness; secondly, because astrologically there is no need. It is not possible to tell from a horoscope whether the person to whom it relates is male or female, because to astrology they are both living individuals full of potential.

BERNARD FITZWALTER

# Part 1

# How the Zodiac Works

# 1. The Meaning of the Zodiac

## Two Times Two is Four; Four Times Three is Twelve

It is no accident that there are twelve signs in the zodiac, although there are a great many people who reckon themselves to be well versed in astrology who do not know the reasons why, and cannot remember ever having given thought to the principles behind the circle of twelve.

The theory is quite simple, and once you are familiar with it, it will enable you to see the motivation behind all the other signs as well as your own. What's more, you only have to learn nine words to do it. That's quite some trick—being able to understand what anybody else you will ever meet is trying to do, with nine words.

It works like this.

The zodiac is divided into twelve signs, as you know. Each of the twelve represents a stage in the life cycle of solar energy as it is embodied in the life of mankind here on our planet. There are tides in this energy; sometimes it flows one way, sometimes another, like the tides of the ocean. Sometimes it is held static, in the form of an object, and sometimes it is released when that object is broken down after a period of time. The twelve signs show all these processes, both physical and spiritual, in their interwoven pattern.

Six signs are used to show the flowing tide, so to speak, and six for the ebbing tide. Aries, Gemini, Leo, Libra, Sagittarius, and Aquarius are the 'flowing' group, and the others form the second group. You will notice at once that the signs alternate, one with the other, around the zodiac, so that the movement is maintained, and there is never a concentration of one sort of energy in one place. People whose Sun sign is in the first group tend to radiate their energies outwards from themselves. They are the ones who like to make the first move, like to be the ones to take command of a situation, like to put something of themselves into whatever they are doing. They don't feel right standing on the sidelines; they are the original have-a-go types. Energy comes out of them and is radiated towards other people, in the same way as the Sun's energy is radiated out to the rest of the solar system.

The people in the other signs are the opposite to that, as you would expect. They collect all the energy from the first group, keeping it for themselves and making sure none is wasted. They absorb things from a situation or from a personal contact, rather than contributing to it. They prefer to watch and learn rather than make the first move. They correspond to the Moon, which collects and reflects the energy of the Sun. One group puts energy out, one group takes it back in. The sun total of energy in the universe remains constant, and the two halves of the zodiac gently move to and fro with the tide of the energies.

This energy applies both to the real and concrete world of objects, as well as to the intangible world of thoughts inside our heads.

A distinction has to be made, then, between the real world and the intangible world. If this is done, we have four kinds of energy: outgoing and collecting, physical and mental. These four kinds of energy have been recognized for a long time, and were given names to describe the way they work more than two thousand years ago. These are the elements. All the energy in the cosmos can be described in the terms of these four: Fire, Earth, Air, Water.

*Fire* is used to describe that outgoing energy which applies to the real and physical world. There are three signs given to it: Aries, Leo, and Sagittarius. People with the Sun in any of these signs find themselves with the energy to get things going. They are at their best when making a personal contribution to a situation, and they expect to see some tangible results for their efforts. They are sensitive to the emotional content of anything, but that is not their prime concern, and so they tend to let it look after itself while they busy themselves with the actual matter in hand. Wherever you meet Fire energy in action, it will be shown as a person whose personal warmth and enthusiasm is having a direct effect on his surroundings.

*Earth* is used to describe the real and physical world where the energies are being collected and stored, sometimes in the form of material or wealth. The three signs given to the element are Taurus, Virgo, and Capricorn. Where Fire energy in people makes them want to move things, Earth energy makes them want to hold things and stop them moving. The idea of touching and holding, and so that of possession, is important to these people, and you can usually see it at work in the way they behave towards their own possessions. The idea is to keep things stable, and to hold energy stored for some future time when it will be released. Earth Sun people work to ensure that wherever they are is secure and unlikely to change; if possible they would like the strength and wealth of their situation to increase, and will work towards that goal. Wherever you meet Earth energy in action, there will be more work being done than idle chat, and there will be a resistance to any kind of new idea. There will be money being made, and accumulated. The idea of putting down roots and bearing fruit may be a useful one to keep in mind when trying to understand the way this energy functions.

*Air* is used to describe outgoing mental energies; put more simply, this is communication. Here the ideas are formed in the mind of the individual, and put out in the hope that they can influence and meet the ideas of another individual; this is communication, in an abstract sense. Gemini, Libra, and Aquarius are all Air signs, and people with the Sun in those signs are very much concerned with communicating their energies to others. Whether anything gets done as a result of all the conversation is not actually important; if there is to be a concrete result, then that is the province of Fire or Earth energies. Here the emphasis is on shaping the concept, not the reality. There is an affinity with Fire energies, because both of them are outgoing, but other than that they do not cross over into each other's territory. Wherever you meet Air energy in action, there is a lot of talk, and new ideas are thrown up constantly, but there is no real or tangible result, no real product, and no emotional involvement; were there to be emotional content, the energies would be watery ones.

*Water* is the collection of mental energies. It is the response to communication or action. It absorbs and dissolves everything else, and puts nothing out. In a word, it is simply feelings. Everything emotional is watery by element, because it is a response to an outside stimulus, and is often not communicated. It is not, at least not in its pure sense, active or initiatory, and it does not bring anything into being unless transformed into energy of a different type, such as Fire. Cancer, Scorpio and Pisces are the Water signs, and natives of those signs are often moody, withdrawn, and uncommunicative. Their energy collects the energy of others, and keeps their mental responses to external events stored. They are not being sad for any particular reason; it is simply the way that energy works. It is quite obvious that they are not showing an outgoing energy, but neither have they anything tangible to show for their efforts, like the money and property which seems to accumulate around Earth people. Water people simply absorb, keep to themselves, and do not communicate. To the onlooker, this appears unexciting, but there again the onlooker is biased: Fire and Air energies only appreciate outgoing energy forms, Earth energies recognize material rather than mental energies, and other Water energies are staying private and self-contained!

We now recognize four kinds of energy. Each of these comes in three distinct phases; if one zodiac sign is chosen to represent each of these phases within an element, there would be twelve different kinds of energy, and that would define the zodiac of twelve, with each one showing a distinct and different phase of the same endless flow of energy.

The first phase, not surprisingly, is a phase of definition, where the energies take that form for the first time, and where they are at their purest; they are not modified by time or circumstance, and what they aim to do is to start things in their own terms. These four most powerful signs (one for each element, remember) are called cardinal signs: Aries, Cancer, Libra, Capricorn. When the Sun enters any of these signs, the seasons change; the first day of the Sun's journey through Aries is the first day of spring, and the Spring equinox; Libra marks the Autumnal equinox, while Cancer and Capricorn mark Mid-summer's Day and the shortest day respectively.

The second phase is where the energy is mature, and spreads itself a little; it is secure in its place, and the situation is well established, so there is a sort of thickening and settling of the energy flow. Here it is at its most immobile, even Air. The idea is one of maintenance and sustenance, keeping things going and keeping them strong. This stage is represented by Taurus, Leo, Scorpio, and Aquarius, and they are called, unsurprisingly, fixed signs. These four signs, and their animal symbols, are often taken to represent the four winds and the four directions North, South, East and West. Their animal symbols (with an eagle instead of a scorpion for Scorpio) turn up all over Europe as tokens for the evangelists Luke, Mark, John and Matthew (in that order).

The final phase is one of dissolution and changes, as the energy finds itself applied to various purposes, and in doing so is changed into other forms. There is an emphasis on being used for the good, but being used up nonetheless. The final four signs are Gemini, Virgo, Sagittarius, and Pisces; in each of them the energies of their element are given back out for general use and benefit from where they had been maintained in the fixed phase. It is this idea of being used and changed which leads to this phase being called mutable.

Three phases of energy, then; one to form, one to grow strong and mature, and one to be used, and to become, at the end, something else. Like the waxing, full, and waning phases of the Moon, really.

The diagram below shows the twelve signs arranged in their sequence round the zodiac. Notice how cleverly the cycle and phases interweave:

(a) Outgoing and collecting energies alternate, with no two the same next to each other;

(b) Physical ebb and flow are followed by mental ebb and flow alternately in pairs round the circle, meaning that the elements follow in sequence round the circle three times;

(c) Cardinal, fixed, and mutable qualities follow in sequence round the circle four times, and yet

(d) No two elements or qualities the same are next to each other, even though their sequences are not broken.

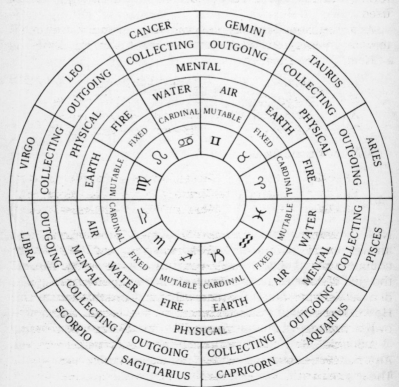

The interweaving is perfect. The zodiac shows all forms of energy, physical and mental, outgoing or incoming, waxing or waning, harmoniously forming a perfectly balanced unity when all the components are taken together. Humanity, as a whole, contains all the possibilities; each individual is a component necessary to the whole.

All this can be a bit long-winded when what you want is some way of holding all that information for instant recall and use, which is where the nine words come in.

If a single word is used for the kind of energy flow, and another two for the element and quality, then they can be used to form a sentence which will describe the way the energy is being used.

As a suggestion (use other words if they are more meaningful to you), try 'outgoing' and 'collecting' for the energy flows.

Next, for the elements:

| Fire  : | activity | (Aries, Leo, Sagittarius) |
| Earth: | material | (Taurus, Virgo, Capricorn) |
| Air   : | communication | (Gemini, Libra, Aquarius) |
| Water: | feelings | (Cancer, Scorpio, Pisces) |

And for the qualities:

| Cardinal : | defining | (Aries, Cancer, Libra, Capricorn) |
| Fixed     : | maintaining | (Taurus, Leo, Scorpio, Aquarius) |
| Mutable : | using | (Gemini, Virgo, Sagittarius, Pisces) |

Now in answer to the question 'What is a Gemini doing?' and answer can be formed as 'He's outgoing, and he's using communication', which neatly encapsulates the motivation of the sign. All that you need to know about the guiding principles of a Gemini individual, no matter who he is, is in that sentence. He will never deviate from that purpose, and you can adapt your own actions to partner or oppose his intention as you please.

A Scorpio? He's collecting, and he's maintaining his feelings. An Arian? He's outgoing, and he's defining activity. And so on. Those nine words, or some similar ones which you like better, can be used to form effective and useful phrases which describe the motivation of everybody you will ever meet. How different people show it is their business, but their motivation and purpose is clear if you know their birthday.

Remember, too, that this motivation works at all levels, from the immediate to the eternal. The way a Taurean conducts himself in today's problems is a miniature of the way he is trying to achieve his medium-term ambitions over the next two or three years. It is also a miniature of his whole existence: when, as an old man, he looks back to see what he tried to do and what he achieved, both the efforts and the achievement, whatever it is, can be described in the same phrase with the same three words.

# 2. The Planets and the Horseshoe

You will have heard, or read, about the planets in an astrological context. You may have a horoscope in a magazine which says that Mars is here or Jupiter is there, and that as a consequence this or that is likely to happen to you. Two questions immediately spring to mind: What do the planets signify? How does that affect an individual?

The theory is straightforward again, and not as complex as that of the zodiac signs in the previous chapter. Remember that the basic theory of astrology is that since the universe and mankind are part of the same Creation, they both move in a similar fashion, so Man's movements mirror those of the heavens. So far, so good. If you look at the sky, night after night, or indeed day after day, it looks pretty much the same; the stars don't move much in relationship to each other, at least not enough to notice. What do move, though, are the Sun and Moon, and five other points of light—the planets. It must therefore follow that if these are the things which move, they must be the things which can be related to the movements of Man. Perhaps, the theory goes, they have areas of the sky in which they feel more at home, where the energy that they represent is stronger; there might be other places where they are uncomfortable and weak, corresponding to the times in your life when you just can't win no matter what you do. The planets would then behave like ludo counters, moving round the heavens trying to get back to a home of their own colour, and then starting a new game.

The scheme sounds plausible, makes a sort of common sense, and is endearingly human; all hallmarks of astrological thought, which unlike scientific thought has to relate everything to the human experience. And so it is: the planets are given values to show the universal energy in different forms, and given signs of the zodiac as homes. Therefore you Sun sign also has a planet to look after it, and the nature of that planet will show itself strongly in your character.

The planets used are the Sun and Moon, which aren't really planets at all, one being a satellite and the other a star, and then Mercury, Venus, Mars, Jupiter, and Saturn. This was enough until the eighteenth century, when Uranus was discovered, followed in the subsequent two hundred years by Neptune and luto. Some modern astrologers put the three new planets into horoscopes, but it really isn't necessary, and may not be such a good idea anyway. There are three good reasons for this:

(a)  The modern planets break up the symmetry of the original system, which was perfectly harmonious;

(b)  The old system is still good enough to describe everything that can happen in a human life, and the modern planets have little to add;

(c)  Astrology is about the relationship between the sky and a human being. An ordinary human being cannot see the outer planets on his own; he needs a telescope. We should leave out of the system such things as are of an extra-human scale or magnitude: they do not apply to an ordinary human. If we put in things which are beyond ordinary human capabilities, we cannot relate them to the human experience, and we are wasting our time.

In the diagram on page 21, the zodiac is presented in its usual form, but it has also been split into two from the start of Leo to the start of Aquarius. The right hand half is called the solar half, and the other one is the lunar half. The Sun is assigned to Leo because in the Northern hemisphere, where astrology started, August is when you feel the influence of the Sun most, especially in the Eastern Mediterranean, where the Greeks and the other early Western civilizations were busy putting the framework of astrology together in the second millenium BC. The Sun is important because it gives light. The Moon gives light too; it is reflected sunlight, but it is enough to see by, and this is enough to give the Sun and Moon the title of 'the Lights' in astrology. The Moon is assigned to Cancer, so that the two of them can balance and complement each other. From there, moving away from the Lights around the circle on both sides, the signs have the planets assigned to them starting with the fastest mover, Mercury, and continuing in decreasing order of speed. Saturn is the slowest mover of all, and the two signs opposite to

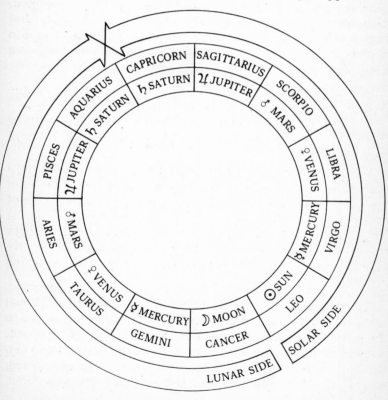

the Lights are both governed by that planet. The reasons for this apparent assymmetry will be explained in a little while. This arrangement is, of course, the horseshoe of the title to this chapter.

The Sun and Moon work in a similar fashion to the outgoing and collecting energies we noted earlier with the twelve signs. The Sun is radiant above all else; energy comes outwards from it, warming and energizing all those around it. Leo people, whose sign is the Sun's, work like this by being at the centre of a group of people and acting as inspiration and encouragement to them all. The Moon reflects the Sun's light, and energies of a lunar kind are directed inwards towards the core of the person. The two energies are necessarily linked; lunar people would starve without the solar folks' warmth, but the solar types need someone to radiate to or their purpose is unfulfilled.

The planets on each side of the horseshoe display their own energies in a solar or lunar way depending on which side of the pattern they are on.

Mercury and Venus form a pair, representing complementary but opposite ideas, which should be familiar by now. Mercury represents difference, and Venus stands for similarity.

Wherever anything new forms that is distinguishable from the background, then Mercury is there making it what it is, highlighting what makes it different. Anything separate is Mercurial, and words, since they are separate and can be strung together into millions of different combinations, are Mercurial too. Mercury is not a long-term influence; it notes things as being different for an instant, and then they become part of the establishment, and something else is new elsewhere. Because 'new' is an instantaneous state—that is, something can only be new once, and for a moment—Mercury is not associated with anything lasting, and its rapid motion as a planet leads to its being associated with the idea of speed. Virgo, Mercury's solar sign, is concerned with the changing of the shape of things ('collecting, using material' in our keyword system), while Gemini, the lunar sign, is concerned with reading and writing, and getting new ideas ('outgoing, using communication').

Venus does the reverse; it looks for that which is similar, finding points of contact to make relationships between common interests and energies. It likes to preserve the harmonies of life, and resents anything which might interrupt them. Love and affection are naturally Venusian, but so is music and all of the Arts, for the harmonies they contain. Expressed in a solar way, Venus is Libra, the maker of relationships; its lunar face is Taurus, emphasizing food and furnishings as things which give pleasure to the individual.

The next pair are Mars and Jupiter. Mars applies force from the outside to impose structure on a disordered universe, while Jupiter expands forcibly from the inside to give growth and wealth, inviting everyone else to join in.

Mars is pure force, energy in a straight line with a direction to go in. Anger and passion are both Martian, and so is lust, because they are all examples of great energy directed towards a given end. Note that Martian force is not necessarily strength, wealth, or know-how, just pure energy, which often boils over and needs controlling. Mars is the power in an athlete, and in an assassin too. It is also the power in a lover, because the urge to create is also the urge to pro-create, and if that energy fulfils its purpose then that creation takes place. Scorpio is its solar side, the power to control and create; in lunar form it is shown by Aries, as energy enjoyed for its own sake by its owner, with no purpose except to express it.

Jupiter is the spirit of expansion from within; not only does it oppose Mars' force from outside, it opposes Mars' physicality with its own mental emphasis. Jupiter develops the mind, then. As it does so, it develops all natural talents of an academic nature, and encourages movement, enquiry and travel to broaden experience and knowledge. The Solar expression of this is Sagittarius, where the centaur symbol is both a wise teacher and a free-roaming wild horse at the same time. Jupiter in a lunar sense is Pisces, where the imagination is developed to a greater extent than anywhere else, but used to provide an internal dream world for the owner's pleasure. Great sensitivity here, but the lunar energies are not of the sort to be expressed; rather other energies are *im*pressed on the Piscean mind.

Saturn is the last of the five planets. He stands alone, and if it is necessary to consider him as paired with anything it is with the Lights as an entity together. The Lights are at the centre of the system; Saturn is at its edge. They are the originators of the energies of the zodiac, and he is the terminator. Everything to do with limits and ends is his. He represents Time, and lots of it, in contrast to Mercury, which represented the instant. He represents the sum total of all things, and the great structures and frameworks of long-term endeavour. In solar form he is Capricorn, the representative of hard work, all hierarchies, and all rulers; in lunar form he is Aquarius, showing the horizontal structure of groups of people within society at different levels. Here he denies the activity of Mars, because society is too big for one person to change against the collective will, and he contains the expansion of Jupiter within himself. Venus and Mercury can neither relate to it nor make it change, because it is always the same, in the end.

The planets show important principles in action, the same as the zodiac does. You have probably noticed that the horseshoe of the planets and the ring of the zodiac say the same thing in a different way, and that is true about most things in astrology. It may be that the two systems interrelate and overlap because they are from the same source: after all, $3+2+2=7$, which is the planet's total, and $3 \times 2 \times 2=12$, which is the signs'. How you assign the elements and qualities, pairs of planets and lights is for you to decide. The joy of astrology, like all magic, is that it has you at the centre, and is made to fit its user's requirements. Now you know the principles, you can use it as you please, and as it seems relevant to you.

# Part 2

# Yourself—and Others

# 3. The Essential Aquarius

All the energy in the zodiac is solar, but that solar energy takes many forms. It is moderated and distributed through the planetary energies until it finally shows in you, the individual. For an Aquarius, the prime planetary energy is that of Saturn; you will be motivated by, and behave in the manner of, the energies of Saturn. To remind yourself of what that means, read the section on Saturn on page 24. As a sign of the zodiac, Aquarius is a Fixed Air sign. Remind yourself what that means by reading page 17. Now we have to see how those essential principles work when expressed through a person and his motivation.

## What it Means to be an Aquarius

You know what it is to be an Aquarius because you are one; but you probably don't know what it is that makes an Aquarius the way he is because you cannot stand outside yourself. You would have to be each of the other eleven signs in turn to understand the nature of the energy that motivates you. This essential energy is in every Aquarian, but it shows itself to different extents and in different ways. Because it is in every single Aquarian, it is universal rather than specific, and universal ideas tend to come in language which sounds a little on the woolly side. You will think that it isn't really about what makes you who you are, because you don't feel like that every day—or at least you think you don't. In fact, you feel like that all the time, but you don't notice it any more than you notice your eyes focusing, yet they do it all the time, and you see things the way you do because of it.

The first thing to note is that the zodiac is a circle, not a line with a beginning and an end. If it were a line, then Aquarius would be towards the far end of it ,but that would be to miss the point; if the zodiac is a circle, then Aquarius is a stage in an endlessly repeating cycle, and we will get a much better idea of what it is if we look to see where it came from.

The sign before Aquarius is Capricorn. Capricorn represents the peak of personal achievement in a material sense. It is where all the effort that you put into your career pays off; it is where your work and worth is recognized and rewarded; it is where you can see and touch your success in terms of money and possessions. The trouble with being at the top, though, is that from there onwards everything is down. To go down by the route you came up is a very disappointing and unsatisfactory procedure, so the only alternative is to take another route down from the top, one whose challenges and rewards are of a different kind. Because Capricorn represents the individual at his most successful, and because Aquarius is beyond that (in the zodiacal sequence), Aquarians don't need to direct their energies towards their own success: they are past that stage. If they aren't concerned with themselves, therefore, they must be concerned with everything that isn't themselves, or society in general. And so they are. Capricorn found himself interested in the structure of his personal existence, and how he could get to the top of it; Aquarius find himself interested in the structures of the society he is part of, and wants to know what it is that links groups of people together. If his interests continue to grow, eventually he may see that society is not only linked, it is interlinked, such that everybody is part of a single whole, containing within itself all possible eventualities, which may or may not choose to take shape. This mind-boggling vision actually belongs to the final stage in the cycle, Pisces: for the moment we must return to Aquarius.

Aquarius is an Air sign, like Gemini and Libra. For all of these signs, the prime energy is mental; ideas, words, and speech are what keeps them going. Aquarius is also a Fixed sign, so here the words and ideas have somehow to be slowed down, kept still. It is the business of Fixed signs to look after what comes their way, caring for it, making it strong and firm, but not adding to it or changing it in any way. How can you do that with ideas?

Like this. When an idea is first created, it is open and flexible. When it is repeated and kept in the same form, it becomes an opinion, something that can be held and quoted by many other people than its creator. If they all decide to keep it as it is, it becomes a belief or a principle of behaviour. If it grows in strength and complexity, it will eventually become a social code of political system, like, say, Marxism. Aquarius is interested in, and feels at home with, this process; it follows the flow of his planetary energies very well. He is interested in any idea or principle which applies to a large number of people at once. In the same way, he is interested in what large numbers of people have to say, or what they feel, rather than the single voice of an individual. Many Aquarians are drawn to politics for these reasons. Many others take up humanitarian causes, such as those of the underprivileged, or perhaps ecological causes, because they are interested in applying a belief, or an ideal, to the whole of humanity, the largest group imaginable.

Not all Aquarians are activists, of course, but they do tend to gather where ideas are kept fixed, stabilized, and prominent. Many are attracted to Science; indeed, it is usually said that the rise of modern scientific thought, and the technology it has brought us, is an Aquarian phenomenon. Possibly so, but what is important about Science is its insistence on provable truth. The idea of a hard, unalterable truth about matter, which will apply to everything, is very Aquarian: it is an idea made fixed, and applied equally to everything; that is, to the widest possible group. Ideas crystallized into principles and then applied to everything are of course rules, as in rules and regulations; they are used to guide the actions of large numbers of people, and usually (it is hoped) for their benefit. All of this is Aquarian thought.

Aquarians care for the world at large, not for themselves. They care for those who have less than the rest, because they sincerely believe that everybody should be equal. They are interested in, and feel comfortable in, any social group; yet they are somehow loners in every group they join, individualists who never quite fit, and noticeably cool in personal relationships. It sounds contradictory: how can it be so?

The answer lies in the horseshoe of the planets, which we looked at earlier on page 24. Aquarius is ruled by Saturn, but is on the lunar side of the horseshoe. Therefore it must be completely opposite to the sort of thing that Capricorn represents, which is on the other end of the horseshoe, yet they must be related in some way because they are adjacent signs in the zodiacal circle, and because they are both expressing Saturn's energy. Saturn will always form structures, and it will always limit expression, because it is opposed to the sources of Light, the Sun and the Moon. These are points worth remembering. Remember, too, that anything which is solar in its nature is personal and individual, whereas anything lunar is general and public. Capricorn's form of structure, then, is a vertical one, a personal ladder to the top of his career; Aquarius's structure is a horizontal one, a firm network of ideas and principles which he uses to help society. Notice that Aquarius's structure is just as rigid as Capricorn's; anybody who protrudes through the network by being higher than his neighbour is seen as a bad thing— Aquarius enforces his horizontality on others, laying low the mighty, elevating the oppressed, until everybody is on the same level. There's militant democracy for you!

Because Aquarius is the lunar version of Saturn, the energies are always applied for the public good, and in a compassionate manner. Lunar light is a caring light, though it is not a light source in itself—it reflects the light it receives from elsewhere. Thus Aquarius needs other people around him before he can exercise his social principles, and so he makes sure that he always has plenty of company. On an individual level, though, Saturn will restrict his response; cool moonlight made even colder by Saturn does not generate personal heat, and Aquarians are thus cool and unemotional creatures at times.

Each sign of the zodiac has a part of the body associated with it, and it is often instructive to think of yourself as functioning generally in the same manner as that part of the body; you provide the function of that organ for the body of society, so to speak. In the case of Aquarius, it is not only the lower leg, symbolizing walking and social activity, but also the nervous system, which is a very close parallel to the systems of social rules which govern our behaviour. Aquarians, then, keep society moving, but they also tell it what it ought to be doing for its own good.

## Early, Middle or Late? The Decanates

Each of the zodiac signs is divided into degrees, like an arc of any other circle. Since a circle has 360 degrees, then each sign must be 30 degrees, since there are twelve signs. Each of the signs is further split into sections of ten degrees, called decanates. There are three decanates in each sign, and the one that your birthday falls in will tell you a little more about how that Aquarian energy actually works in you as an individual.

*First decanate (20–29 January)*
This is the purest form of Aquarius. There is a double helping of Saturnine energy here, expressed as a very strong denial of the individual. Almost all of the energy is turned outwards, away from the person, and towards society at large. Not surprisingly, all forms of politics are assigned to this part of the sign, especially those where the views of the majority are the important ones. Hence, democracy in all its forms, from the House of Commons to a revolutionary Socialist party somewhere in the Third World, belongs here. Where the views of only one person matter, such as in a monarchy or under dictatorship, then astrologically that is assigned to Leo, and this part of Aquarius is of course directly opposed to that. If you were born in this decanate, you are likely to have very firm political views. You may not express them openly, but you will have your own ideas

on the way things should be done, and you will be very angry with people who, in your view, are doing the wrong thing. There is a tendency for you not to see any point of view but your own— an 'unusual thing for an Air sign, but if anything can restrict communication, double Saturn can. What matters to you are principles—individual excuses or failures to serve the cause don't concern you at all. You can be hard on yourself for the sake of something you believe in, so you don't see why other people can't do the same.

## Second decanate (30 January–9 February)

Here the harsh energy of Saturn is mingled with the lighter and faster energies of Mercury. Mercury will always insist on communication of some kind, wherever it is, and it is at its best in the exchange of ideas. It also works at close range; it doesn't usually have enough power to be effective over great stretches of time or distance. As a result, the energies of the Aquarian from this decanate find themselves working on the level of personal friendships rather than on the grander scale of political theories. All forms of personal friendship are given to this decanate; if your birthday is here you will be a firm believer in the theory of 'It's not what you know, it's who you know that matters'. You will have lots of friends, in lots of different circles—each one of them gives you an opportunity to make a different kind of association, and you will like that. 'Association' is a very Aquarian word, and it applies specifically to this part of the sign. There are two sorts of association: the first is any group of people who share a common view, which must be a familiar enough example of Aquarian thought by now, and the second is a relationship between two people with a very low emotional content. You like that sort of thing: even when you are close to somebody, you like to feel that you are still a little bit apart, still private to yourself.

## Third decanate (10–19 February)

The last decanate has Saturn's force softened and made more flexible by Venus's influence. This isn't altogether unwelcome—

the end of the sign is near, and Pisces, the next sign, is very soft indeed, so if the transition isn't to be too hard the last degrees of Aquarius will need to be a lot less strict. This is the humanitarian end of Aquarius, the part that supports every sort of good cause from animal rights to campaigning for the release of political prisoners. As usual with Aquarius, the vision is universal; you find it a lot easier to support the cause of all mistreated animals than to take a personal interest in one particular example. That doesn't mean that you don't feel involved; it means that you feel equally involved for all cases, that the principle behind the abuse is what really upsets you, and that you are naturally drawn towards any sort of organization or association which dedicates itself to these causes on a large scale. This decanate also concerns itself with the public appearance of things, and how they are seen by the world at large; if you have a job in public relations or media communications with a large corporation, then you are definitely in the right place!

# Three Phases of Life: Aquarius as Child, Adult, Parent

## *The Aquarian Child*
The Aquarian child shows his character rather later than some of the other signs; it is always in the nature of Saturn to be slow in its action, and it has no affinity with extreme youth and infancy. Aquarian toddlers are usually self-contained and reasonably happy little people, neither over-expressive nor over-demanding. This is entirely to do with Saturn, of course; they will feel, even at that early age, that they are their own private people. They do have interests which are different from those of all their friends, though, and these will make themselves apparent quite early on—the Aquarian independence asserting itself. Sometimes Aquarian children seem to attract trouble to themselves at school, a process which mystifies their parents and teachers. It is actually to do with the fact that schools are hierarchical institutions, with subject teachers, house or class tutors, and

senior pupils in a well-defined power structure. Aquarian children will refuse to recognize this, and will try to bypass this system wherever possible. As pupils, they are usually better at logical and scientific subjects such as maths and physics, and particularly poor at expressive Arts subjects, with the notable exception of music. Music provides expression for an Aquarian in a way nothing else can, and it is very important to him because of that. The only other way the young Aquarian shows what he feels is through his friends; his opinions are an important influence on their views, and so rather than show his feelings as an individual, he shows them by using the group. What this means to his teachers and parents is that if he changes his company he is angry about something, and is surrounding himself with the people necessary to express that feeling. When given a chance to argue, in class debate, or in an essay, he will show how clearly he thinks, and also how important the principles of things are to him—it is his understanding of the idea rather than its practical application which will develop into the political views of his adult life.

## The Aquarian Adult

The grasp of the underlying principles of things which he developed in his childhood stays with the Aquarian throughout his life. He is proud of his ability to see the thought behind the action, and proud, too, of his own capacity for logical appraisal. More than anything else, the fully-grown Aquarian is rational: to him, everything has to be there for a reason, and when he has discovered the reason he will be satisfied. Like the Sagittarian, the Aquarian is very confident of himself, but for very different reasons. Most people are a little worried when they find themselves in a new situation, because they don't trust themselves to be able to handle anything that comes their way; the 'collecting' signs are particularly prone to this worry. Sagittarius is confident in himself because he has optimism and belief; he believes that things will work out well each time. Aquarius is confident in himself because he has logic—he is sure of what he knows, he is happy with his own opinion of himself, and he is sure that he will be able to analyze anything he meets in terms of one universal principle or another. In addition, of course, the Aquarian knows that nothing he meets will actually affect him in any way: his habit of keeping himself at a slight remove from all of his activities means that he remains constant, and unaffected by any of them. The adult Aquarian never trust his emotions, or any emotional response he may have to a given situation; emotions are far too individual and personal as far as he is concerned, completely opposed to common opinion or universal scientific principles.

It's not easy ro see the impersonal Aquarian from the outside. Because they are so helpful, so friendly, so good with their advice, and so interested in the welfare of others, they appear to be radiating warmth. The logical assumption from that is that they must be in themselves warm, but it is not so—it is just that their energy is directed away from themselves. They are clever and logical, caring and inventive; but always, at the heart of things, alone.

## The Aquarian Parent

Aquarian parents are models of fairness. They are never the sort who say 'Do what I say, not what I do' or 'Because I say so, that's why!' They always explain to their children the reasons and principles behind what they want them to do, and hope that the children will choose to do things their parents' way because they have seen that it is for the best reasons. Whenever a child has a grievance, it will find a sympathetic and impartial ear with an Aquarian parent. Aquarian parents are often seen as being very modern, and untroubled by the different values of the generation beneath them. The reasons are simple, and nothing to do with modernity: firstly, the Aquarian parent is quite sure of his own opinions, and those of a child are unlikely to cause him to change them; and secondly, he can see the reasons behind the apparently outrageous behaviour of his teenage children, and understand that it is essentially the same as his own behaviour was at that age.

If Aquarian parents have a fault, it is that they are not

comfortable expressing themselves in an emotional way. Some children work on a very high emotional level, and demand the same in return: it is the only way that they can communicate. This is particularly true if the child is from a Water sign. In these cases there is a communication problem which the parent understands quite well, and the onus is on him to do something about it, but he will refuse. Aquarian parents don't want their children to be emotional and changeable; they want them to be self-contained and independent like themselves, and they tell them so. In creating a communications gap between themselves and their children, of course, they are well on the way to achieving their goal.

# 4. Aquarius Relationships

## How Zodiacal Relationships Work

You might think that relationships between two people, described in terms of their zodiac signs, might come in 144 varieties; that is, twelve possible partners for each of the twelve signs. The whole business is a lot simpler than that. There are only seven varieties of relationship, although each of those has two people in it, of course, and the role you play depends on which end of the relationship you are at.

You may well have read before about how you are supposed to be suited to one particular sign or another. The truth is usually different. Aquarians are supposed to get on with Geminis and Librans, and indeed they do, for the most part, but it is no use reading that if you have always found yourself attracted to Virgos, is it? There has to be a reason why you keep finding Virgos attractive, and it is not always to do with your Sun sign; other factors in your horoscope will have a lot to do with it. The reason you prefer people of certain signs as friends or partners is because the relationship of your sign to theirs produces the sort of qualities you are looking for, the sort of behaviour you find satisfactory. When you have identified which of the seven types of basic relationship it is, you can see which signs will produce that along with your own, and then read the motivation behind it explained later on in more detail in

'The Aquarian Approach to Relationships' and the individual compatibility sections.

Look at the diagram on page 16. All you have to do is see how far away from you round the zodiacal circle your partner's Sun sign is. If they are Cancer, they are five signs in front of you. You are also, of course, five signs behind them, which is also important, as you will see in a little while. If they are Scorpio, they are three signs behind you, and you are three signs in front of them. There are seven possibilities: you can be anything up to six signs apart, or you can both be of the same sign.

Here are the patterns of behaviour for the seven relationship types.

*Same sign*
Somebody who is of the same sign as you acts in the same way that you do, and is trying to achieve the same result for himself. If your goals permit two winners, this is fine, but if only one of you can be on top, you will argue. No matter how temperamental, stubborn, devious, or critical you can be, they can be just the same, and it may not be possible for you to take the same kind of punishment you hand out to others. In addition, they will display every quality which really annoys you about yourself, so that you are constantly reminded of it in yourself as well as in them. Essentially, you are fighting for the same space, and the amount of tolerance you have is the determining factor in the survival of this relationship.

*One sign apart*
Someone one sign forward from you acts as an environment for you to grow in. In time, you will take on those qualities yourself. When you have new ideas, they can often provide the encouragement to put them into practice, and seem to have all your requirements easily available. Often, it is this feeling that they already know all the pitfalls that you are struggling over which can be annoying; they always seem to be one step ahead of you, and can seemingly do without effort all the things which you have to sweat to achieve. If the relationship works well, they are

helpful to you, but there can be bitterness and jealousy if it doesn't.

Someone one sign back from you can act as a retreat from the pressures of the world. They seem to understand your particular needs for rest and recovery, whatever they may be, and can usually provide them. They can hold and understand your innermost secrets and fears; indeed, their mind works best with the things you fear most, and the fact that they can handle these so easily is a great help to you. If the relationship is going through a bad patch, their role as controller of your fears gets worrying, and you will feel unnerved in their presence, as though they were in control of you. When things are good, you feel secure with them behind you.

*Two signs apart*

Someone two signs forward from you acts like a brother or sister. They are great friends, and you feel equals in each other's company; there is no hint of the parent-child or master-servant relationship. They encourage you to talk, even if you are reticent in most other company; the most frequently heard description of these relationships is 'We make each other laugh'. Such a partner can always help you put into words the things that you want to say, and is there to help you say them. This is the relationship that teenagers enjoy with their 'best friend'. There is love, but it does not usually take sexual form, because both partners know that it would spoil the relationship by adding an element of unnecessary depth and weight.

Someone two signs behind you is a good friend and companion, but not as intimate as somebody two signs forward. They are the sort of people you love to meet socially; they are reliable and honest, but not so close that things become suffocatingly intense. They stop you getting too serious about life, and turn your thoughts outwards instead of inwards, involving you with other people. They stop you from being too selfish, and help you give the best of yourself to others. This relationship, then, has a cool and a warm end; the leading sign feels much closer to his partner than the trailing sign does, but they are both satisfied by the relationship. They particularly value its chatty quality, the fact that it works even better when in a group, and its tone of affection and endearment rather than passion and obsession.

*Three signs apart*
Someone three signs in front of you represents a challenge of some kind or another. The energies of the pair of you can never run parallel, and so must meet at some time or another. Not head on, but across each other, and out of this you can both make something strong and well established which will serve the two of you as a firm base for the future. You will be surprised to find how fiercely this person will fight on your behalf, or for your protection; you may not think you need it, and you will be surprised that anybody would think of doing it, but it is so nonetheless.

Someone three signs behind you is also a challenge, and for the same reasons as stated above; from this end of the relationship, though, they will help you achieve the very best you are capable of in a material sense. They will see to it that you receive all the credit that is due to you for your efforts, and that everyone thinks well of you. Your reputation is their business, and they will do things with it that you could never manage yourself. It's like having your own P.R. team. This relationship works hard, gets results, and makes sure the world knows it. It also looks after itself, but it needs a lot of effort putting in.

*Four signs apart*
Someone four signs forward from you is the expression of yourself. All the things you wanted to be, however daring, witty, sexy, or whatever, they already are, and you can watch them doing it. They can also help you to be these things. They do things which you think are risky, and seem to get away with them. There are things you aim towards, sometimes a way of life that you would like to have, which these people seem to be able to live all the time; it doesn't seem to worry them that things might go wrong. There are lots of things in their life which frighten you, which you would lie awake at nights worrying

about, which they accept with a child's trust, and which never go wrong for them. You wish you could be like that.

Someone four signs behind you is an inspiration to you. All the things you wish you knew, they know already. They seem so wise and experienced, and you feel such an amateur; luckily, they are kind and caring teachers. They are convincing, too. When they speak, you listen and believe. It's nice to know there's somebody there with all the answers. This extraordinary relationship often functions as a mutual admiration society, with each end wishing it could be more like the other; unfortunately, it is far less productive than the three-sign separation, and much of its promise remains unfulfilled. Laziness is one of the inherent qualities of a four-sign separation; all its energies are fulfilled, and it rarely looks outside itself for something to act upon. Perhaps this is just as well for the rest of us.

*Five signs apart*

Someone five signs ahead of you is your technique. You know what you want to do; this person knows how to do it. He can find ways and means for you to do what you want to be involved in, and he can watch you while you learn and correct your mistakes. They know the right way to go about things, and have the clarity of thought and analytical approach necessary if you are to get things clear in your mind before you get started

Someone five signs behind you is your resource. Whenever you run out of impetus or energy, they step forward and support you. When you're broke, they lend you money, and seldom want it returned. When you need a steadying hand because you think you've over-reached yourself, they provide it. All this they do because they know that it's in their best interest as well as yours, to help you do things, and to provide the material for you to work with. You can always rely on them for help, and it's nice to know they will always be there. They cannot use all their talent on their own; they need you to show them how it should be done. Between you, you will use all that you both have to offer effectively and fully, but it is a relationship of cooperation and giving; not all the zodiac signs can make it work well enough.

*Six signs apart*

Someone six signs apart from you, either forwards or backwards, is both opponent and partner at the same time. You are both essentially concerned with the same area of life, and have the same priorities. Yet you both approach your common interests from opposite directions, and hope to use it in opposite ways. Where one is private, the other is public, and where one is self-centred, the other shares himself cheerfully. The failings in your own make-up are complemented by the strengths in the other; it is as if, between you, you make one whole person with a complete set of talents and capabilities. The problem with this partnership is that your complementary talents focus the pair of you on a single area of life, and this makes for not only a narrow outlook, but also a lack of flexibility in your response to changes. If the two of you are seeing everything in terms of career, or property, or personal freedom, or whatever, then you will have no way to deal effectively with a situation which cannot be dealt with in those terms. Life becomes like a seesaw; it alternates which end it has up or down, and can sometimes stay in balance; but it cannot swing round to face another way, and it is fixed to the ground so that it does not move.

These are the only combinations available, and all partnerships between two people can be described as a version of one of the seven types. It must be remembered, though, that some of the roles engendered by these dispositions of sign to sign are almost impossible to fulfil for some of the signs, because their essential energies, and the directions they are forced to take by the planets behind them, drive them in ways which make it too difficult. To form a relationship based on sharing and acceptance is one thing: to do it when you are governed by a planet like Mars is somethings else. Even when the relationship can form, the sort of approach produced by, say, Jupiter, is a very different thing from that produced by Venus.

The next thing you must consider, then, is how you, as an Aquarius, attempt relationships as a whole, and what you try to find in them. Then you must lay the qualities and outlook of

each of the twelve signs over the roles they must play in the
seven relationship types, and see whether the pair of you
manage to make the best of that relationship, or not.

The seven relationship types are common to all the signs,
relating to all the other signs. You can use your understanding of
them to analyse and understand the relationship between any
pair of people that you know, whether or not they are Aquarian;
but to see how the characters fit into the framework in more
detail, you will need to look at the individual compatibilities, of
which just the Aquarius ones are given in this book.

## The Aquarius Approach to Relationships

An Aquarian wants a number of things from a relationship, but
few of them are the same as what most other people want. What
he particularly *doesn't* want is to lose himself in another person,
or to lose himself in the unreal effects of being in love, or to
create something better than he could be on his own from a
combination of his own talents and his partner's.

He doesn't want to prove himself sexually, and he feels no
need to produce children as a duty to his ancestors, in a way that,
for example, a Capricorn often does. He is not trying to express
his inner feelings as an attempt to communicate his existence to
another person, either.

Most of these things are expressions of the energies of the
inner planets, Venus and Mars; Aquarius works on a more
impersonal level than that, provided by the slowest mover of
them all, Saturn. Much of the business of personal expression is
due to solar energy showing itself; Aquarius is on the lunar half
of the horseshoe, though, and so that need, too, is absent.
Whatever an Aquarian wants from a relationship must be very
cool, very controlled, and very realistic. That doesn't mean
unenjoyable, but it does mean that the fantasy of love has no
meaning for him.

Almost everything an Aquarian does can be explained in
musical terms. Why this should be so is not clear: perhaps it has
something to do with the fact that music is a universal language,

and that it has rhythm and measure (rhythm is a Lunar thing, measure is Saturnine). Whatever the reason, when trying to grasp the Aquarian way of doing things, a musical metaphor is often very helpful, and here is no exception. The Aquarian approach to relationships is like slow, cool jazz.

Relationships, to an Aquarian, must contain an exchange of thoughts and ideas. He is an Air sign, and so conversation and company are of much greater importance to him than physical satisfaction or any kind of possessive emotional bonding. He needs to stay circulating around society at large; to devote himself to one person and deny himself the company and stimulation he gets from everybody else he knows is something he is anxious to avoid. Love affairs are often exclusive; the two partners spend a lot of time with each other, but very little in the company of other people. Indeed, once a partnership is recognized by their friends, the couple are usually left alone. This is a serious problem for an Air sign. Earth and Water people may like to be left alone, but not Air signs. Of the Air signs, Librans like to work on a one-to-one basis, but not Aquarians. They want their social environment to stay just the way it always was; it's part of being a Fixed sign.

Friendships are the best relationships for an Aquarian, and he usually has a lot of them. A friendship is usually shared, in that the relationship is often part of a wider social group, and that suits the sign very well. Friendships are also a mutual benefit arrangement, in that friends are usually able to perform small services for each other, and being able to put energy outwards for the benefit of somebody else unable to do it for himself is a very Aquarian thing. There is also the question of status: friends are implicitly equals, which is certainly not the case in a teacher-pupil or employer-employee relationship, and often not the case in a husband-wife relationship, or that between two lovers. Remember that Aquarius is highly egalitarian; he detests any kind of relationship where one partner is in a position of power over the other. Saturn is a great leveller.

Finally, though friendships can be deep and satisfying, they don't have to be devoted: you can leave a friendship as a part-time arrangement, and pick it up again some time later if you wish. You can't do that with a love affair or a marriage. Aquarians have a need to be on their own at times, to re-order their thoughts, and to feel solitude; it is an important part of them, and if they are in a relationship which makes it difficult for them to have this time on their own then they are troubled.

All of these things make friendship the best kind of relationship for Aquarians. They know that it needn't be close or demanding, and they know that it will be flexible and communicative. It isn't as powerfully satisfying as an intimate relationship, but quantity can compensate for quality in some cases, and the Aquarian prefers to have many friends in different circles than one life partner.

Friendship usually happens on a one-to-one basis. Light though it is in comparison to marriage, it can be too intimate for Aquarians; they are happy to leave all personal involvement to their Air element colleagues the Librans, and have instead devised something unique to themselves: group friendship. There isn't a word for this process, but it is very easy to recognize. It is the relationship enjoyed by a dozen young men who go to the same pub every Friday night. It is the relationship enjoyed by all the girls in an office when they all go out together for a meal and then on to a disco. Everybody in the group contributes to the feeling of friendliness, and everybody feels that they have the support and affection of everybody else, but nobody is particularly closely tied to any other individual in the group, and so they don't feel emotionally tied or committed. Each person also feels that he is still an individual. The great feature of this sort of group relationship is that emotional support is generated without deep or personal passion. Aquarians feel very much at home in this sort of environment, as do young adults, who lack either the confidence or the inclination to form deep and lasting relationships, but who nonetheless need to feel that they are appreciated.

Aquarians are the originators of this behaviour pattern. They are an essential part of every group, and a major provider of ideas and energy within it, but they are somehow separate from it at the same time, maintaining that sense of isolation which is so characteristic of the sign.

The Saturnine part of Aquarius makes him constant and caring in all circumstances, and that includes love affairs and marriages: the problem, as far as the other partner is concerned, is to convince the Aquarian that such a personal and individual partnership is what he wants—he would rather just be friends. That is not to say that no Aquarians feel compelled to marry or fall in love, but the pure influence of the Sun in Aquarius doesn't incline them that way; the fact that they do so is because of other features of their horoscope. Aquarius itself needs variety, and mental rapport, not physical passion or personal devotion.

# Individual Compatibilities Sign by Sign

All relationships between the signs work in the ways described earlier in 'How Zodiacal Relationships Work' (p. 35). In addition to that, descriptions of how an Aquarian attempts to form a relationship with someone from each of the twelve signs are given below. I have tried to show not what an Arian, for example, is like, but what an Aquarian sees him as, and how he sees you. Each individual Aries looks different, of course, but their motivation is the same, and these descriptions are meant to help you understand what you are trying to do with them, and how they are trying to handle you. As usual, the words he and his can be taken to mean she and her, since astrology makes no distinctions in sex here.

### Aquarius-Aries

On the surface, this relationship has a lot to recommend it. Arians are strong and active, and they like to be where the action is; they're not the sort to stay at home and read a book. They are also highly independent and self-motivating; they don't need somebody else to help them get the best out of their life. You may thing that because you, too, are of an independent turn of mind, and enjoy the social scene, that you would be ideally suited. Not so: you are indeed both independent, and the result is that you don't really need each other.

Arians are very active, but also very physical. They are at their best when they are actually doing something, and using their muscles to do it—their particular kind of planetary energy needs to be expressed through the functioning of their bodies. When they are not physically active, they don't know what to do with themselves. Not surprizingly, they try to spend as much time as they can in action.

Their universe is physical; they like real problems which they can overcome through hard work and sweat. Yours is the world of ideas—the principles of the matter are more important to you than how they are put into action, and you will have a great deal of difficulty understanding the Arian's insistence on doing it himself. He likes to be personally involved; only if he actually does things for himself can he get anything out of the experience. In this respect he is very different from you, because you don't mind at all if somebody else does the deed.

He is independent, like you are, but more than that he is individual. He is concerned entirely for, and with, his own existence. It isn't that he is selfish; it is simply that other people are outside his comprehension. All of his values come from what he feels as he does things, and he can't understand anything that is not in his own direct experience. He can't understand why other people aren't the same as he is either. Such a sense of being alone and individual, the centre of existence, is very alien to you. You are the representative of the idea of doing things in groups; you see everything as part of a larger society, whose members share the same hopes and ambitions. You like to think yourself independent and aloof, but only within the framework of a larger group. Aries doesn't have to recognize the existence of any group, or even of society; he is independent, full stop.

You see him as a tremendously energetic person, full of confidence, and eager to get stuck in to whatever there is to be done. You are slightly in awe of his keenness for getting his hands dirty; somehow you can't bring yourself to get so involved with anything. He seems childishly naïve, in some respects; his opinions seem to be formed instantaneously, without any thought for what other people might say, and he seems never to consider what might lie behind some of the things he gets involved in.

He sees you as lively and sociable, but oddly unwilling to say what you really mean. What he likes about you is that you can always see the reasons behind things, and the helpful way you explain these to him makes him feel that you have his interests at heart. For somebody as helpful and as friendly as you, he will do anything he can, like a child who is eager to please.

You like being useful to Arians—it's part of how you work. In return, they give you their enthusiasm and energy, and the warmth your cold Saturnine heart needs.

You may not make the best of lovers, because you just can't muster enough heat to match the Arian's fiery Mars. You have strength and stamina of your own, and a cool sense of the erotic and the tantalizing, but Aries isn't subtle enough to appreciate you on that level. He likes it hot, physical, and right now, please.

As business partners you should be very successful. You can do the thinking, and he can do the work—between you, you should go a long way.

Marriage is a difficult subject for either of you to think about. It stops the Arian from rushing off and doing things on his own, and it means that you have to commit yourself to one person. You both need movement, though of different kinds, and marriage may not suit either of you. Even if you're sure that it's what you want, you may have to wait a very long time before you find an Arian who feels the same way.

### Aquarius-Taurus

This pairing isn't very easy, at least not in its initial stages. You are so very different in almost every way. You would like to be out with your friends, but the Taurean would rather stay at home. You welcome new ideas, because they exercise your mind, but the Taurean hates them, because he likes things to be predictably constant. Above all, your definition of wealth is in ideas, but theirs is in possessions.

The thing that will strike you most strongly about Taureans is their insistence on familiarity and security. They like to be in familiar surroundings, doing things the way that they have always done them; anything which takes them into unfamiliar territory is quite frightening to them. If they can't avoid being away from home, they will try to impose their own routines on their new surroundings; the best example is the Taurean on a package holiday who tries to get a cup of tea wherever he goes.

Security is a physical thing to a Taurean; he gets real comfort from his possessions. He is also comforted by what he wears, and particularly by what he eats; the idea that mere possessions could improve your opinion of yourself is likely to fascinate you, but you won't really understand it. They seem to be so easily satisfied, in your eyes; you wish they had a broader outlook, one which took in the needs of more people than just themselves, and which saw beyond the simple acquisition of material security.

From the other point of view, they see you as kind and fair, but cold and distant. You don't seem to *enjoy* yourself enough, in their opinion. You are as comfortable in the company of your friends as they are in the company of their favourite possessions, and they can appreciate that, but you don't seem to get any real enjoyment from the things you have, and they think that's rather sad. Still, as long as you don't interfere with what they have, and don't threaten their territory, then they won't mind too much.

There is one area in which you have a common interest: music. Not all Taureans are musical, nor all Aquarians for that matter, but most of you are. The reasons for this are, as usual, linked to the planets which govern your signs. Taurus is looking for the comfort of a pleasant environment for all of his senses. This includes his hearing; he will be very fond of tunes he knows well. He is fonder of pure melody than you are, though you probably have a better understanding of rhythm and time. Together, Venus and Saturn produce harmony (in a musical sense); a shared interest in music may well help form a friendship between you.

A friendship between you works best if you let yourself become an addition to his group of friends; that way, you get a wider circle of acquaintance, and he doesn't lose anything with which he was familiar before, which is the best arrangement for both of you.

An affair between you could be better than you might think; you are both strong, and both have stamina. Your emotional coolness will hurt him, though, as his passion will surprise you. His possessiveness will bother you, too—you like, and indeed need, variety. You will both need to compromise; you are more flexible than he is, though, so it's really up to you, if you think it's worth it.

The same problems occur in a marriage. They will want to do things their way or not at all, and you will have to be very persistent if you are to get them to make any major changes. Lack of commitment isn't the problem—it's a simple unwillingness to change, and you will find that quite wearing.

As business partners you will be very supportive to each other, but the partnership will lack the spirit of enterprise necessary to make new projects successful. Why? Because the Taurean is wary of anything new, and because you won't let yourself get involved in them to the extent necessary to ensure success.

### Aquarius-Gemini

This is a very comfortable and entertaining relationship for you to be in. The two of you are both Air signs, and that means that you are both more concerned with words and ideas than with the actions they imply, and neither of you like getting bogged down in the emotional side of things. Gemini is, in fact, very dry indeed emotionally: almost without deep feelings at all. As far as you are concerned, this isn't a problem, and anyway you are both so busy talking to each other and laughing at each other's jokes that the subject hardly ever crops up.

When it does, you will notice something about the Gemini that you find a little distasteful: he is unprincipled. Or, as he would no doubt put it, he is more flexible in his thinking. To him, an idea is something to play with; he likes to turn it around in his mind, see if he can get it to mean something else, see if he can make new things from it. To experiment in this way with words themselves is part of the Gemini way of life—a thing has only the meaning that you give it for that instant, and nothing is ever the same for all time. Such an approach is a little shocking to you— ideas are almost sacred things to you, to be strengthened rather than dismantled, and to be used for the guidance of mankind generally rather than for the amusement of an individual. Ah, well, that's the difference between the Mutable Air sign and the Fixed Air sign. It would probably do you good to be able to take your beliefs less dogmatically, and to be able to play with them in the Gemini's fashion; after all, everything must go from the Fixed phase of its existence to the Mutable eventually, as we noted on page 15.

For his part, Gemini sees you as just a little bit dull. Don't be upset: he just likes his people lively and quick-witted, that's all, with an eye for a bargain and a bit of a game on the side. Your big talent, that of being friendly to everybody, and being the driving force behind any group you care to join, is not important to him. He can talk to anybody he likes, and be friendly, too, if it suits him; all the Air signs can, and so it's not an impressive thing, in his view. Groups of people, and particularly the beliefs and opinions they all share, don't matter to him one way or the other; Geminis prefer to work on an individual basis anyway, and have little time for fixed opinions. He is willing to listen to what you have to say, though, particularly if he hasn't heard it before—his appetite for novelty is even greater than yours. He uses you as a source of new ideas, which he then plays with and disassembles to see if there is anything else interesting contained in them. This is a one-way process—don't expect him to contribute anything in return. If he did, would you listen? If you listened, would you trust what he had to say?

The friendship between you is based largely on the fact that you both enjoy talking; you enjoy talking to each other, and you enjoy talking to other people, too, which means that you can keep up the social circulation that you both need without threatening the relationship between you. Obviously, this is a good thing. The other good thing about this pairing is that neither of you expects, or offers, any sort of deep emotional attachment; you are 'just good friends'—literally! The disadvantage of this is that you don't support each other much, but then neither of you expects it, so that isn't so bad.

As lovers, you are quite well matched. Neither of you likes things too intense, and both of you like a sense of humour in your sex life. Gemini is likely, if anything, to be too lightweight even for Aquarius, in the final analysis: he would probably rather talk and play games than get serious about anything.

In marriage, as in business, the big question is whether you would ever get anything done. You like each other well enough, and you can keep each other amused for ever, but he is so easily sidetracked by anything new; you will have to allow for this.

## Aquarius-Cancer

This, along with the Pisces pairing, is probably the most difficult relationship of all from your point of view. Almost everything there is about a Cancerian is exactly opposed to your own point of view, and you will find it very difficult to get to know them thoroughly enough for you to understand why they feel the way they do. This is a great pity in many ways; both of you would like to care for the other very much, since caring is what you both do best—but in very different ways.

You are, as you know, most comfortable in a crowd of people, and especially if they are your friends. People expect to bump into you socially; they know that if they go to a party the chances are that you will be there, chattering away to all and sundry. You also know that you have a private, interior personality, which is known only to you, and never communicated to anyone else at all—not ever. The public face is friendly and helpful; the private person may not be. Whatever he is, he has a very serious view of himself, and he likes his own company and his own thoughts best. When his own thoughts look likely to take up too much of his time, the private person puts on a public face, and goes out with his friends, or does something which helps other people; anything to turn his attention away from himself.

Can you imagine a person whose interior is all that they have? Can you imagine a person as private as you are inside, but who has no public personality to hide behind, and whose sense of insecurity makes them shy and nervous when they have to deal with more than a few people at once? Cancer is like that.

You are similar in many respects. Both of you, for instance, need other people to bring out the best in you, to allow you to communicate your planetary energies fully. You like to think that you can be of use to society as a whole; Cancer likes to think that he can be of use to his immediate family and friends. You work on a much larger scale, of course—and in time as well as space, because you are often thinking about the far future when you adopt a course of action—but you are both trying to do the same thing: that is, to benefit other people, and to be appreciated for that.

Cancer's urge is to protect and nourish, whereas yours is more impersonal, and in that you can see the biggest difference between you: the difference between the emotional response and the logical response. Aquarians have a distrust of emotional responses; they are random things, and they can appear to distort the truth from time to time. You are always concerned that things should be fair and true, without bias of any kind, and you will suppress your own emotional responses to eliminate any possible bias in your own judgements. Not that you could do otherwise, of course: the suppression of emotion is as good a description of the action of Saturn on the Lunar side of a person as you could ever devise.

Cancer is all emotion, no logic. Emotional security is all he is interested in. He will do anything to protect himself and his family against what he sees as a hostile world, and he values the affection they give in return.

You will see them as defensive shy worriers; they see you as friendly but impersonal. A friendship between you will take some time to get going—first you have to gain their confidence, and then you have to trust them with your internal emotions. It may not be possible for you to do this; if you manage it, you can be sure that Cancer will look after you with a devotion you could not have imagined. What you can offer them is an example of caring on a bigger scale; if they can understand it, they will take it as seriously as you do. It may not be possible for them to widen their viewpoint sufficiently to take in your ideas; though they will appreciate the ideals behind your opinions, they are likely to find them too cold emotionally.

As business partners, on the other hand, you could do very well indeed; each of you supplies what the other one lacks. Of course, being business partners keeps things on the unemotional basis which you like best; as lovers, things would be the other way round. You would be completely unable to reply to the Cancerian's emotional demands, and quite unused to the intensity at which they would conduct the affair anyway. You would feel not only lost, but trapped as well—a most uncomfortable situation for you, and one perhaps best avoided.

If in time, you learned how to trust and respond to each other, you might consider marriage. It wouldn't be easy: you need to be on your own, and they need to cling. A lot of adjustments would have to be made.

### Aquarius-Leo

Leo is the sign of the zodiac you find it easiest to dislike. The feeling is entirely mutual, but provided that neither of you take yourselves too seriously you can be quite good friends—something that isn't at all unknown with signs opposite each other.

The reason for your antipathy is actually political. Not party political—though it could be—but to do with your principles of equality. Leos have an inbuilt feeling of superiority. It seems to them that they are somehow better than the rest of us—grander, larger than life, more important altogether. As a result they often lead extravagant and flamboyant lifestyles, surrounding themselves with lots of friends, and admirers. It often seems as though a Leo's life is one long party, and that his social life is similar to that of a king and his court.

It is this that irritates you. In your view, everybody should be the same. When you see the Leo being the centre of attention, you want to give somebody else a turn. You want to see him made to look silly, or somehow humbled; anything to stop him being so self-important. Note that you don't want a chance to wear the crown yourself—you just don't want him to either.

What you haven't seen is that although you may not need the Leo to put some light into your life, *other people do*. His energy and warmth are given out for free; he is an essential part of any group of people—he is its centre. A great many people like being around Leos, and to bring him down to the same level as the rest of us would not only harm him, it would deprive us of the good he does.

Leo is, if nothing else, personal. He is very fond of simply being himself. You, of course, are impersonal: what you do, or what you represent, is far more important to you than who you are. You therefore see him as selfish and opinionated, without much care for the future or for that of anyone else; he sees you as another face in the crowd, but one whose high principles mean that he has forgotten how to enjoy himself. You will see, I hope, that you are both wrong; you are trying to define the other person's existence in terms of what has value for you but not for him.

If you are prepared to let him be at the centre of things, and take the leading role, then things will be better automatically, because he will be in his natural place. Your place is around him and by him, but not at the centre. You can still enjoy the company of the rest of your friends; indeed, the group will be brighter for having the Leo at its centre. All you have to do is accept his version of himself, and not try to limit him. You are both very sociable people, and have plenty to contribute to any group in your own ways; if you spend your time at war with each other nobody will benefit.

Whether or not you succeed as lovers depends on whether you let yourself accept what he has to offer. Leos are genuinely warm and generous people; you are unused to such open affection, and may not allow yourself to be warmed by him. If you do, you may feel that you have to offer something in return.

Not so: Leos are content if you enjoy what they offer. All you have to do is tell him how much you enjoy it.

As business partners you will do best if Leo is seen as the boss. He may not be the boss, but he must be seen that way. He does do things in an expansive way, but he's no fool: Leos are much better organized than most people expect, and are quite capable of looking after a number of things at once. He will appreciate, in private at any rate, your cool appraisals of the situations you face.

For a marriage partner, you could do a lot worse: Leo will have to be lord in his own home, but he will provide a feeling of well-being and warmth which you could never produce on your own.

## Aquarius-Virgo

This is another difficult one, though less so than the Cancer pairing. At least there are no emotional problems here; Virgo usually keeps his feelings to himself unless he is very angry, and even then it will be due to some rule being broken rather than an irrational outburst of feelings. You feel at home with his kind of mentality.

You are both very reasonable people: you both have a fondness for reasoned scientific thought. Virgo likes to know what the correct way of doing anything is supposed to be, and you like to do things for the right reasons; there are plenty of similarities there.

Virgo is wonderfully practical, in your eyes. You have always been better at handling ideas than the practicalities of their application, but Virgo is one step further down yet—he is the sort of person who understands the machines that do the work. To you, this interest and knowledge about things at their smallest and most basic level is as fascinating, and as remote, as molecular biology. You are full of interest and admiration, but you know that you could never do this sort of thing for yourself.

In Virgo, you see your own idealism translated to the material world. Virgos think things through first. They decide what has to be done, and then do it in the best way possible, making the best use of the tools and time they have available. Nothing is done haphazardly, and everything is to the highest possible standard, no matter what it costs in effort. Virgoans are not lazy, and they are not selfish either: they seem to exist to do things for other people, and in the best possible way.

You like all this. You like his ability to see into things—it matches your own. The problems start when you realize that looking into things is the end of the matter as far as he is concerned. His close-up view of the details of things never takes in the whole picture. What really matters to you, the universal application of ideas, has little interest for him. Ideas aren't practical things, as far as he's concerned, and his view of things doesn't really lend itself to considering more than one person at a time. The problem is one of incompatibility, but with an interesting twist. You have similar approaches to things, but you work in different worlds, and on different scales: there is almost no common ground.

A friendship between you isn't impossible, by any means. You are capable of being friendly to anyone, because you are an Air sign, and although he is an Earth sign, he is Mutable, which speeds him up to somewhere near your pace. In addition, he is ruled by Mercury, the planet of words; he doesn't talk like a Gemini, but he's chatty enough. You seem to want to talk to each other—your aims and methods interest each other, and your analytical approaches do too.

Though you are suited to each other, you are not really suited to being lovers. Both of you are cool emotionally, and neither of you can generate the heat and passion necessary for an affair to be self-sustaining; obviously it just isn't that important to you. It isn't really the right situation for your talents: Aquarius does better being publicly rather than privately appreciated, while Virgo's often critical comments can destroy a relationship before it has had time to establish itself.

As with the Cancer partnership, this one is good from a business point of view, and for the same reasons: you each provide what the other lacks. Add your talents for seeing the larger situation to the Virgo's capacity for hard work and you have a very productive combination.

A marriage between you would be as productive as a business partnership, but you might have some trouble generating enough emotional warmth; you could grow apart from each other.

### Aquarius-Libra

This is probably the easiest of your relationships. Libra is interested in the same sort of thing as you are—that is, talking to people—and he goes about it in a similar sort of way. He is as friendly and as outgoing as you are, and as much at home in a social setting. If anything, you are too much like one another!

What first attracts you to a Libran is his lightness and pleasantness. He seems to have a knack of putting you at your ease, and of saying things which you want to listen to. What he says isn't necessarily new or different, but he seems to say it in a way that you find agreeable, and you are left with the impression that he is a very nice person to know. He is genuinely interested in being your friend, but he never makes any demands on you.

This is exactly the sort of thing you want. What you are reacting to here is Air sign energy, the same stuff as you yourself are made of. The great thing about it, as far as you are concerned, is that it is light, bright, and flexible, and never gets bogged down in the dark waters of emotional demands and expectations. It is essentially a surface thing, and doesn't touch the inner layers of the person at all. Some people (Cancerians, for instance) would find this a major drawback—they would want the relationship to come from the core of the person, not the surface—but it suits you well, and the Libran too.

A relationship between you, then, is bright and friendly, and full of new ideas. Neither of you gives yourself completely to the other, but that doesn't matter at all; the relationship wouldn't be able to stand the extra weight if you did, and neither of you would want the responsibility of the other one's inner self anyway.

What you have that the Libran doesn't is the ability to work on the grand scale. As you get to know a Libran, and watch him in company, you will see that he is dedicated to forming personal relationships on a one-to-one level. He has lots of individual friends, and he treats each one separately as though he were the only other person in the world. You have lots of friends together; you see them together, you have fun with them together, and you prefer to see them all at once; individual, one-to-one relationships are sometimes more intense than you would like.

What he has that you don't is charm. That doesn't mean that you're tongue-tied and clumsy, but Libra's charm is so strong that it becomes a physical force, shown as grace and style. He doesn't seem to be able to make a clumsy move; he always looks attractive, whatever he wears; his sense of colour and style is perfect. Librans can make wherever they are a nicer place to be, just by being there; you can't do that, and if you tried, it would come out as a better way of life instead of a more enjoyable one. They're not the same thing.

If your friendship develops into an affair, you need have no fear; it will be every bit as enjoyable as your original relationship. Most affairs have a heavy emotional ingredient, and you are rightly wary of that, but Libra is different. For him, an affair is a thing of Romance with a capital R; it becomes a game where roles are played and enjoyed in place of real feelings and commitment, and you can enjoy that as much as he does. Sexually you are both playful, and not too demanding: you are a good match for each other.

In business together you are not quite such a good idea, unless you are in some kind of public relations or personnel business. You would both rather sit and talk to people than get on with the serious business of working, and since neither of you are Earth signs you will lack the ability to convert work into money the way they do.

Marriage would be a good thing, from your point of view. Your Libran will make sure you have an attractive life together and a beautiful home, but they need your sense of organization to stop them being lazy.

*Aquarius-Scorpio*
You may be attracted to a Scorpio. There is nothing to be worried

about: everybody is attracted to a Scorpio. They are that sort of person.If you decide to form some sort of a relationship with them, though, you would be well advized to think about what you are taking on: they work in a very different way from you. They see everything in terms of emotions, like Cancerians and Pisceans. They will rearrange the rules of the game to suit themselves, something you would never do. Finally, they will never, ever, lose or let go. They may be a lot more than you want.

It would be a reasonable thing to assume that, since you are both Fixed signs, you would both be trying to do the same sort of thing. It is true, to a certain extent, but the difference in the elements you represent does its best to disguise the fact. You are both trying to keep things going—but there the similarity ends. For your part, you would like to understand and be part of the common interest that makes different people become friends and associates. The Scorpio, however, would like to understand and control the desires and concerns that make different people become friends and associates. Try it this way: if all of society were a forest, and all the people trees, then the Aquarian would want to see the topmost leaves waving as the wind blew over them, and the Scorpio would want to control the underground river that their roots all drank from.

In your view, people act the way they do because they all have a shared belief; they act for the best motives, and so things will get better in the end for us all. In the Scorpionic view, people act the way they do because they all have desires and fears; if these are understood, they can be controlled by the Scorpio, and he need fear nothing from any of them.

Your view is upwards and outwards; his is inwards and downwards. He is at least as penetrating and analytical as you are, but he is looking for different things. Universal principles and humanitarian ideas don't interest him; he is working to provide extra information for himself. He is envious of your understanding of society as a whole—he has to spend too much time with individuals, he thinks, and he would like to develop your talent for seeing the larger scene. He could do with some of your social skills, too, or so he thinks: he has a reputation for being either secretive or irresistibly sexy, and he would actually like to be anonymously pleasant on the surface whilst remaining secretly powerful underneath. I know that your social skills don't actually work that way, but that's how he sees you.

You see him as magnetically attractive, and very powerful. He seems to have the same sort of mental control that you have, and the same cold logic; he also seems to have the physical power that you lack, but held in check, controlled, in the way you are sure that you would if you had that power. It's just how you see him, in fact, because he isn't really like that. He doesn't have your cold logic at all; he has a hot, irrational temper, held down and controlled by cold logic, and he daren't let it go. It is a much more explosive situation than yours; he certainly can't allow himself the luxury of being kind to others in the way you can—he needs all his energy to look after himself.

A friendship between you is bound to be something of a battle. It will only take you a few minutes to realize that they are interested primarily in themselves, in a way that you are not, and that they will happily use whatever you have to offer them for their own profit, without offering anything in return. You need exchange of ideas and friendship, and this isn't it: as soon as you are able to free yourself from the scorpion's claws you will be off. The best way to do it is to be even cooler than usual; Scorpio reacts to your emotional heat, and if there isn't any you are invisible to him.

You are most unsuited as lovers, unless you are specifically trying to experience passion, possessiveness, jealousy, obsession, and all the other high emotions which usually have so little meaning to you. Scorpios take sex very seriously—much too seriously to talk about it, as you would like to do.

The major obstacle to your business success is that Scorpio won't trust you not to betray him unless he feels that he controls you. You are above that sort of thing, and the suggestion that you are unprincipled annoys you. In any case, you would rather not be in business with him than be controlled by him.

Marriage would be another battleground. Eventually you might understand him, and make allowances for him; in return you will have a partner whose drive and sensuality will really fire your imagination. You would stay with each other—Fixed signs do—but he will always be suspicious of anything new or different. Can you live with that?

## Aquarius-Sagittarius

The last of the Fire signs is likely to make your best friend. The partnership forms very easily; only Libra is easier, and this one is probably better for you in the long run.

It must have seemed up to now that there is no other sign of the zodiac where the mind is interested in ideas for their own sake in the way that yours is. You must also have been disappointed to find that almost everybody else is concerned either with themselves and their own welfare, and in the odd instances where this is not so (Libra) attention seems to be focused on two or three people at the most.

Sagittarius can change all that. Sagittarians are so confident about themselves, and their ability to cope with anything that Life can throw at them, that they give almost none of their attention to their own well-being. Instead, they direct their energy upwards and outwards, and give themselves entirely to the quest for, and the spreading of, knowledge. Sagittarians, like you, are interested in the truth that lies behind everything.

It all sounds too good to be true; here at last is the partner with whom you can swap ideas and experiences all day long! It is true, and it is even better than you had dared hope: Sagittarius thinks in a different way from you, but a way which is complementary to your own. You can take a positive interest in the difference in your approaches, even!

The difference is a simple one. You work from the outside inwards, defining a general principle in a logical manner, and applying it to everybody equally. The approach is very scientific. Sagittarius works from the inside outwards, from an unshakeable *belief* in what must be right. You will be tempted to label this sort of knowledge, probably saying that it is 'intuitive'. You are wrong: Sagittarians are *inspired*. They look for knowledge in everything, and they find it. What's more, when they find it, it is pretty much as they knew it would be—as though they knew it all already. This process is endlessly absorbing to you: you could sit and watch it for hours. Sagittarians like to have somebody to talk to, to share their discoveries with them, but that person has to be used to big ideas, and they have to be able to think clearly. You are exactly the right person for the job.

Friendship between you is almost instantaneous. You have so much that you want to tell each other! They are more emotional than you are, but because the dominant emotion is happy enthusiasm, you enjoy them being that way. They see you as a bit on the reserved side, but they are determined to make you laugh if they can: they feel sure that you are capable of it!

As lovers, you will probably laugh a lot. Sagittarians have a silly and boisterous side to them, but it is so obvious they don't take things seriously that you don't feel trapped by becoming involved. They also like to stay fancy-free, if they can; since you like to be independent too, you are unlikely to complain.

In business you could be unstoppable. Sagittarius has the drive you sometimes lack, and you have the overall sense of organization that gets lost in his enthusiasm. You make a great team. The same holds true for marriage; the only question there is whether you can both sacrifice your independence to the extent of actually getting married! If you do, you won't regret it, but it will be a difficult thing for either of you to do. You may well decide that you are happy enough with each other as you are— and not bother.

## Aquarius-Capricorn

This is a very difficult one from your point of view, much more difficult than the other way round. The sign that is behind you in the zodiacal sequence usually represents all the things that you have left behind, so to speak: people from that sign are living examples of the sort of qualities you would like to think that you have grown out of.

The problem is similar to the one you have with Leos—it is to do with status and position. Capricorns take their station in life very seriously. They work very hard and for a very long time, denying themselves all the comforts that the other signs find so enjoyable, but keeping their sights fixed the whole time on the position they want to be in, at the top of the tree. When they have made it to the top, they want the world to see where they are, and to be impressed by it. At any stage in their career they would like you to notice how much better off they are than you, and to admire the things that show you their status: their fine house, the BMW in the drive, and so on. They never give anything away; every ounce of their energy is devoted to furthering their career, making a life of lasting quality and material comfort for themselves and their families.

You are strongly opposed to almost everything the Capricorn does, and particularly for the reasons that he does it. You know that you could do all of that if you tried—all you have to do is use your Saturnine energy the way he does—but you also know that if you did, you would be slipping backwards. The only thing that you agree with in his methods is the fact that he is prepared to push himself very hard and to work long hours for what he really believes in; you are like that too.

Everything the Capricorn wants out of life has a price tag on it. His goals are all material; he doesn't give himself a lot of time to ponder on ideas and principles. This isn't surprising; he is an Earth sign, after all. All the things you want out of life are without price, and most of them are not physical at all; they are qualities or beliefs, like friendship, truth, and justice.

He can see your talent for analysis, and your ability to lead and motivate large numbers of people. He is sure that he could make a lot of money with that sort of ability, and he can't see why you don't. He can see that you have a large number of friends, but he can't see why you don't use them as business contacts. Above all, he can't see why you don't want to be better than the next man, or to have a bigger car.

You are going to have a lot of trouble trying to explain yourself to him. He isn't very receptive to ideas; he prefers practical examples. He's no good at catching nuances from your speech, either, or at being imaginative. Most difficult of all, perhaps, is his highly traditional point of view; the sort of things that you consider logical, effective, and innovative are to him 'simply unthinkable—just not done'.

You are only going to be friends if one of you is crossing over into the other's territory (that is, if you are relapsing into material comfort, or if he is being unusually progressive), or if you are working together for the same organization, such as a political party. Without shared goals, you will fight. All business partnerships between you will have to be that way, too. You will both be able to work long and hard if you have a common target, but if that isn't the case you will criticize him for his mercenary motives and his lack of imagination, and he will feel resentful.

Marriage, because it often has shared goals, isn't a bad idea. Both of you prefer to work over a long period of time, and neither of you expects instant results. Your personal relationship could be a bit cold and dry, though—two Saturn people don't generate much heat.

As lovers? Well, you like things lighter and more playful than Capricorn, but he is stronger than you. He has a better-developed sense of humour, too, even if it is something of an acquired taste. You like things cool and off-beat, though, so once you are used to each other it would probably work very well.

## Aquarius-Aquarius

Forming a relationship with somebody from your own sign is both a good and bad thing. You know more or less what you're getting, which is a good thing, but you are not getting anything fundamentally different from yourself, which means that you don't have to stretch your capabilities to accommodate them, and so you don't make as much progress as you might.

In this case, the union is by no means as bad as it might be: in fact, it is one of the best of the same-sign pairings. The odd thing about it is that although it is rather slow to get going, it improves as time goes on. If it survives the initial stages and becomes something with a long-term element in it, such as a marriage, then it may turn out to be the most satisfying relationship of the twelve.

The reasons for that are, of course, entirely to do with Saturn lord of Time; only another Saturnine person can provide suppor and companionship at the level you want it (that is, not ver intense) for the length of time that you want it (for years) Aquarian and Capricorn are the only choices for that kind o long duration, and Capricorn doesn't always see things you way, as we have noted.

To begin with, your relationship will be very friendly an sociable. This is hardly surprising; both of you are virtuall professional socializers, and if you can't function on a socia basis then you can't function anywhere. You can, in fact, g quite a long way on just that level: you needn't offer or deman each other's trust or affection—you could keep things light an sociable, chatting away whenever you saw each other, going t the cinema together, or things like that.

When you deepen the relationship you will find that you hav a deeper understanding than you had perhaps supposed. Eac of you will need some time away from the other, some time when you can be alone with yourself and your thoughts. You nee frequent changes of scene and company, and you don't lik being in the company of any one person for too long. Who els would ever understand that but another Aquarian? Anyone from the other eleven signs would take it as a signal to end th relationship if you wanted a few days on your own, but you don have to explain it to another Aquarian. Better still, you wil understand the same behaviour in them.

You make some strange demands on a close relationship. Th partner must be similar to you, but different. You must bot enjoy the company of others, and be part of the crowd, but at th same time you must feel that you are both separate and differen from the crowd in some way. Your partner must be close to you and take the relationship seriously, but not be attached to you Above all, he must let you go your own way, and alone if that' the way you want it from time to time. Only another Aquarian ca do all that.

Friendship is no problem: what about an affair? It is likely t be very enjoyable for both of you. If you let your imagination get to work you can have a wonderful time, similar to the sort of affair you would have with a Libran. There is the merest hint of wistful sentiment in the Aquarian soul, which could be persuaded, in circumstances such as these, to blossom into a pale and delicate romance. There is also a dry sort of electricity in you, the same power which makes you so zealous in support of your egalitarian ideals. If this power can be expressed sexually, then the two of you could make a crackling, sparky, free-form relationship, something very different from the sort of stuff the rest of the zodiac gets up to. What you have to guard against is taking your relationship too seriously: then Saturn makes your loving dull and earnest, and you lose all the fun from it.

In business together you become an extension of each other, but that doesn't mean that you are any more successful than you were separately. You will still need somebody practical and somebody creative: somebody non-Aquarian, in other words.

In a marriage, you will get better as time goes on. Your differences, and your efforts to remain different from and independent of each other will keep you from becoming dull and inflexible. That way, the essential Aquarian spirit, which needs to stay mentally active, keeps going, and keeps you going, too.

## Aquarius-Pisces

The relationship you have with the sign which is the next one on from you is always rather strange. You want so much to be part of their world, to progress to their stage in the cycle, but somehow it always seems to be unattainable. They know you very well, of course; they have already been where you are, so to speak, and they know that they can sink back into you when things get tough.

Pisces seems impossible for you to understand. You pride yourself on being able to handle ideas, and being an Air sign ought to give you a certain adaptability, but Pisceans are something else altogether. Whenever you try to pin them down, they slip away. Whenever you think that you understand what they mean, you find they meant something else. There doesn't seem to be anything constant about them; your attempts to define the principle on which they work get you nowhere.

The truth of the matter is that they don't work on any principl
at all; they take on the behaviour of what surrounds them. Thes
people react emotionally to everything and everybody the
meet, and they construct a pattern of behaviour from thos
responses.

To be so open to external influence is staggering to you; yo
are the complete opposite. Though you take in all that you se
and hear, very little of it has any real effect on you; you analys
it, examine it, and remain unaffected by it for the most par
Pisceans are not nearly so controlled. They positively enjo
being swept away by an intensity of feeling or experience—the
live life in Technicolour, digital stereo sound, and probably
number of other processes yet to be invented.

It is difficult for the two of you to form a relationship tha
satisfies you both at once: if things are light and cool enough fc
you then they are unlikely to be intense enough for the Piscear
Your social life could be the answer; Pisceans get as muc
enjoyment from their friends as you do, though in a differer
fashion. Another good idea is probably music, that key to you
own emotions; if you have a shared interest in that, it will serv
as a starting point.

A deep relationship between you is bound to have i
problems. Remember that the Piscean will pick up and reflec
whatever you project; if you want to be on your own for a while
then the Piscean will feel completely isolated and abandonec
because he will have absorbed your emotional state. You wi
have to be careful. Episodes like this will enable you to se
perhaps, why he is so difficult to pin down; if he absorbs th
emotions of wherever he is, then he must have some means c
distancing himself from those he doesn't want to be near. It is h
self-regulation mechanism, in the same way as being cool an
logical is yours.

As lovers, you could have a wonderful time, or not: it is reall
up to you. He will be able to recognize and reflect the slighte
emotion from you, so it all depends on how much you want t
put into it. The softer and more romantic you are, the warmer

response you will produce in the Piscean. Sexually, Pisceans are capable of making any fantasy into reality—how imaginative are you between you?

In business you would be better than you might think. Let the Piscean absorb some of your logical approach; in return, pay attention to the way he absorbs the feeling of what's going on. When he says that the time is right for a product or a service, it usually is.

If you were married, the Piscean would keep things from becoming too static. They may be emotional, but they're not obsessive, so any rows would soon be over.

# Part 3

# Your Life

# 5. The Year within Each Day

You have probably wondered, in odd moments, why there are more than twelve varieties of people. You know more than twelve people who look completely different. You also know more than one person with the same Sun sign as yourself who doesn't look anything like you. You also know two people who look quite like each other, but who are not related, and do not have birthdays near each other, so can't be of the same Sun sign. You will have come to the conclusion that Sun signs and astrology don't work too well, because anyone can see that there are more than twelve sorts of people.

You will also have wondered, as you finished reading a newspaper or magazine horoscope, how those few sentences manage to apply to a twelfth of the nation, and why it is that they are sometimes very close to your true circumstances, and yet at other times miles off. You will have come to the conclusion that astrology isn't all that it might be, but some of it is, and that you like it enough to buy magazines for the horoscopes, and little books like this one.

It might be that there is some other astrological factor, or factors, which account for all the different faces that people have, the similarities between people of different Sun signs, and the apparent inconsistencies in magazine horoscopes. There are, indeed, lots of other astrological factors we could consider, but one in particular will answer most of the inconsistencies we have noticed so far.

It is the Ascendant, or rising sign. Once you know your Ascendant, your way of working, your tastes, your preferences and dislikes, and your state of health (or not, as the case may be). It is perhaps of more use to you to consider yourself as belonging to your Ascendant sign, than your Sun sign. You have been reading the wrong newspaper horoscopes for years; you are not who you thought you were!

You are about to protest that you know when your birthday is. I'm sure you do. This system is not primarily linked to your birthday, though. It is a smaller cogwheel in the clockwork of the heavens, and we must come down one level from where we have been standing to see its movements. Since astrology is basically the large patterns of the sky made small in an individual, there are a number of 'step-down' processes where the celestial machinery adjusts itself to the smaller scale of mankind; this is one of them.

Here's the theory:

Your birthday pinpoints a particular time during the year. The Sun appears to move round the strip of sky known as the zodiac during the course of the year. In reality, of course, our planet, Earth, moves round the Sun once a year, but the great friendly feature of astrology is that it always looks at things from our point of view; so, we think we stand still, and the Sun appears to move through the zodiac. On a particular day of importance, such as your birthday, you can see which of the zodiac signs the Sun is in, pinpoint how far it has gone in its annual trip round the sky, and then say 'This day is important to me, because it is my birthday; therefore this part of the sky is important to me because the Sun is there on my special day; what are the qualities of that part of the Sun's journey through the zodiac, and what are they when related to me?' The answer is what you usually get in a horoscope book describing your Sun sign.

Fine. Now let's go down one level, and get some more detail. The Earth rotates on its own axis every day. This means that, from our point of view, we stand still and the sky goes round us once a day. Perhaps you hadn't thought of it before, but that's how the Sun appears to move up and across the sky from sunrise to sunset. It's actually us who are moving, but we see it the other way round. During any day, then, your birthday included, the whole of the sky goes past you at some time or another; but at a particular moment of importance, such as the time that you were born, you can see where the Sun is, see which way up the sky is, and say, 'This moment is important to me, because I was born at this time; therefore the layout of the sky has the same qualities as I do. What are the qualities of the sky at this time of day, and what are they when related to me?'

You can see how you are asking the same questions one level lower down. The problem is that you don't know which bit of the sky is significant. Which bit do you look at? All you can see? All that you can't (it's spherical from your point of view, and has no joins; half of it is below the horizon, remember)?

How about directly overhead? A very good try; the point in the zodiac you would arrive at is indeed significant, and is used a lot by astrologers, but there is another one which is more useful still. The eastern horizon is the point used most. Why? Because it fulfils more functions than any other point. It gives a starting point which is easily measurable, and is even visible (remember, all astrology started from observations made before mathematics or telescopes). It is also the contact point between the sky and the earth, from our point of view, and thus symbolizes the relationship between the sky and mankind on the earth. Finally, it links the smaller cycle of the day to the larger one of the year, because the Sun starts its journey on the eastern horizon each day as it rises; and, if we are concerned with a special moment, such as the time of your birth, then the start of the day, or the place that it started, at any rate, is analogous to the start of your life. Remember that you live the qualities of the moment you were born for all of your life; you are that moment made animate.

The point in the zodiac, then, which was crossing the eastern horizon at the time you were born, is called the Ascendant. If this happened to be somewhere in the middle of Gemini, then you have a Gemini Ascendant, or Gemini rising, whichever phrase you prefer. You will see that this has nothing to do with the time of year that you were born, only with the time of day.

Different signs are on the horizon at different times according to where you live, as you can see. This is because of the difference in latitude. If you live in between the places given, you can make a guess from the values here. To compensate for longitude, subtract twelve minutes from your birthtime if you live in Glasgow, Liverpool or Cardiff; ten minutes for Edinburgh or Manchester, and six minutes for Leeds, Tyneside, or the West Midlands. *Add* four minutes for Norwich.

Have a look at the diagram opposite, which should help explain things. If two people are born on the same day, but at different times, then the Ascendant will be different, and the Sun and all the other planets will be occupying differentparts of the sky. It makes sense to assume, then, that they will be different in a number of ways. Their lives will be different, and they will look different. What they will have in common is the force of the Sun in the same sign, but it will show itself in different ways because of the difference in time and position in the sky.

How do you know which sign was rising over the eastern horizon when you were born? You will have to work it out. In the past, the calculation of the Ascendant has been the subject of much fuss and secrecy, which astrologers exploit to the full, claiming that only they can calculate such things. It does take some doing, it is true, but with a few short cuts and a calculator it need only take five minutes.

Here is the simplest routine ever devised for you to calculate your own Ascendant, provided that you know your time of birth. Pencil your answers alongside the stages as you go, so you know where you are.

1. Count forwards from 20 January to your birthday: 20 January is 1, 21 January is 2, and so on.
   Total days:  . . . . . . . . . . . . . . . . . . *9* . . . . . . . . . . . . . .
2. Add 122 to this. New total is:  . . *122* . . . . . . . . . . . . . .
3. Divide by 365, and then
4. Multiply by 24. Answer is now:  . . . . . . . . . . . . . . . . . . . . . . .
   (Your answer by now is between 0 and 24. If it isn't, you have made a mistake somewhere. Go back and try again).
5. Add your time of birth, in 24-hour clock time. If you were born at 3 p.m., that means 15. If you were born in Summer Time, take one hour off. If there are some spare minutes, your calculator would probably like them in decimals, so it's 0.1 of an hour for each six minutes. 5.36 p.m. is 17.6, for example. Try to be as close as you can. New total is: . . . . . . . . . . . . .
6. If your total exceeds 24, subtract 24. Your answer must now

be between 0 and 24. Answer is: . . . . . . . . . . . . . . . . . . . . .

7. You have now got the time of your birth not in clock time, but in sidereal, or star, time, which is what astrologers work in. Page 72 has a strip diagram with the signs of the zodiac arranged against a strip with the values 0 to 24, which are hours in star time. Look against the time you have just calculated, and you will see which sign was rising at the time you were born. For example, if your calculated answer is 10.456, then your Ascendant is about the 16th degree of Scorpio.

## What Does the Ascendant Do?

Broadly speaking, the Ascendant does two things. Firstly, it gives you a handle on the sky, so that you know which way up it was at the time you entered the game, so to speak; this has great significance later on in the book, when we look at the way you handle large areas of activity in your life such as your career, finances, and ambitions. Secondly, it describes your body. If you see your Sun sign as your mentality and way of thinking, then your Ascendant sign is your body and your way of doing things. Think of your Sun sign as the true you, but the Ascendant as the vehicle you have to drive through life. It is the only one you have, so you can only do with it the things of which it is capable, and there may be times when you would like to do things in a different way, but it 'just isn't you'. What happens over your life is that your Sun sign energies become adapted to specifically express themselves to their best via your Ascendant sign, and you become an amalgam of the two. If you didn't, you would soon become very ill. As an Aquarius with, say, an Arian Ascendant, you do things from an Aquarius motivation, but in an Arian way, using an Arian set of talents and abilities, and an Arian body. The next few sections of the book explain what this means for each of the Sun/Ascendant combinations.

Some note ought to be made of the correspondence between the Ascendant and the actual condition of the body. Since the

Ascendant sign represents your physical frame rather than the personality inside it, then the appearance and well-being of that frame is also determined by the Ascendant sign. In other words, if you have a Libra Ascendant, then you should look like a Libran, and you should be subject to illnesses in the parts of the body with a special affinity to that sign.

## The Astrology of Illness

This is worth a book in itself, but it is quite important to say that the astrological view of illness is that the correlation between the individual and the larger universe is maintained. In other words, if you continue over a long period of time with a way of behaviour that denies the proper and necessary expression of your planetary energies, then the organ of your body which normally handles that kind of activity for your body systems will start to show the stresses to you. A simple example: Gemini looks after the lungs, which circulate air, and from which oxygen is taken all over the body. Gemini people need to circulate among a lot of people, talking and exchanging information. They act as the lungs of society, taking news and information everywhere. They need to do this to express their planetary energies, and society needs them to do this or it is not refreshed, and does not communicate. You need your lungs to do this, too. Lungs within people, Geminis within society: same job, different levels. If you keep a Gemini, or he keeps himself, through circumstance or ignorance, in a situation where he cannot talk or circulate, or where he feels that his normal status is denied, then he is likely to develop lung trouble. This need not be anything to do with a dusty atmosphere, or whether he smokes, although obviously neither of those will help; they are external irritants, and this is an internal problem caused by imbalance in the expression of the energies built into him since birth. In the sections which follow, all the observations on health are to do with how the body shows you that certain behaviour is unbalancing you and causing unnecessary stress; problems from these causes are alleviated by listening to yourself and changing your behaviour.

## Your Ascendant

*Aries Ascendant*

If you have Aries rising, you are an uncommon individual, because Aries only rises for about fifty minutes out of the twenty-four hour day. You must have been born in the middle of the morning, or else you have got your sums wrong somewhere.

What you are trying to do with yourself is project an Aquarius personality through an Arian vehicle. You will always be trying to do things faster than anybody else, and this can lead to hastiness and a certain degree of accident-proneness. What you see as the correct way to do things involves immediate action by the most direct method, to secure instant, and measurable, results. You feel that unless you are directly and personally responsible for doing things, then they cannot be done, not only because you believe that only you can do them properly, but because you get no satisfaction from letting anybody else do anything. Personal experience of everything is the only way you learn; reading about it, or watching it, does nothing for you.

You are likely to have headaches as a recurring problem if you push yourself too hard, and you should watch your blood pressure too. Mars, ruling Aries, is a strong and forceful planet, and it is bound to get you a little over-stressed at times. You are also likely to have problems digesting things properly. Astrologically, all illnesses apply to your external condition as well as your internal condition, so think carefully; when your head aches you are banging it too hard against a problem which cannot be overcome that way, and when you are not digesting properly, you have not understood the implications of what you have taken on. In both cases, allow time to think and consider.

*Taurus Ascendant*

You were born somewhere near noon if you have Taurus rising. If you are a January Aquarian a Taurean Ascendant will also make you prominent in your chosen career, whatever it may be. Taureans are generally fond of food—did you arrive in time for lunch, or were you a little early? You should have all the Taurean physical characteristics: quite thick-set, big around the neck and shoulders sometimes, and with large hands. You should have a broad mouth, and large eyes, which are very attractive. You should also have a good voice—not only as a singing voice, but one which is pleasant to listen to in conversation too.

The Taurean method for getting things done is to look forward to, and then enjoy, the material reward for one's efforts. It is part of Taurean thinking that if you can't touch it, buy it, own it or eat it, it isn't real and it isn't worth much. You will also be concerned to keep what is yours, not to waste your energies on what won't gain you anything or increase your possessions, and not to attempt anything which you don't think you have more than a chance of achieving.

Taureans do have taste; not only taste for food, which they love, but artistic taste, which they develop as a means of distinguishing things of value which they would then like to acquire and gain pleasure from owning. Unlike the Capricorn way of doing things, which values quality because it is valued by others, Taureans enjoy their possessions for themselves. The drawback to the Taurean approach is the lack of enterprise, and the unwillingness to try things just for the fun of it.

Taurean Ascendant people have throat and glandular problems, and all problems associated with being overweight. They can also have back and kidney problems caused as a result of an unwillingness to let things go in their external life. A lighter touch is needed in the approach to problems of possession; shedding unwanted or outworn things in a desirable process.

## Gemini Ascendant

If you have a Gemini Ascendant you were born somewhere in the middle of the day; if you were born before noon you should achieve prominence in your chosen career. You should have expressive hands and a wide range of gestures which you use as you speak (ask your friends!) and you are perhaps a little taller than average, or than other members of your family. Gemini Ascendant people also have dark hair, if there is any possibility of it in their parents' colouring, and quick, penetrating eyes which flash with amusement and mischief; Gemini Ascendant women have very fine eyes indeed.

The Gemini approach to things, which you find yourself using, is one in which the idea of a thing is seen as being the most useful, and in which no time must be lost in telling it to other people so that they can contribute their own ideas and responses to the discussion. The performance of the deed is of no real importance in the Gemini view; somebody else can do that. Ideas and their development are what you like to spend time on, and finding more people to talk to, whose ideas can be matched to your own, seems to you to offer the most satisfaction.

There are two snags to the Gemini approach. The first is that there is a surface quality to it all, in which the rough outline suffices, but no time is spent in development or long-term experience. It may seem insignificant, but there is some value in seeing a project through to the end. The second snag is similar, but is concerned with time. The Gemini approach is immediate, in that it is concerned with the present or the near future. It is difficult for a Gemini Ascendant person to see farther than a few months into the future, if that; it is even more difficult for him to extend his view sideways in time to see the impact of his actions on a wider scene. Both of these things he will dismiss as unimportant.

Gemini Ascendant people suffer from chest and lung maladies, especially when they cannot communicate what they want to or need to, or when they cannot circulate socially in the way that they would like. They also have problems eliminating wastes from their bodies, through not realizing the importance of ending things as well as beginning them. In both cases, thinking and planning on a broader scale than usual, and examination of the past to help make better use of the future, is beneficial.

## Cancer Ascendant

You were born in the afternoon if you have your Ascendant in Cancer and your Sun in Aquarius. The Cancerian frame, through which you project your energies, may mean that you appear rounder and less lean-framed than other Aquarians. Your energies are in no way diminished; in fact, you are likely to be even more determined to get things right. Your face could be almost cherubic, and you could have small features in a pale complexion with grey eyes and brown hair. The key to the Cancer frame is that it is paler than usual, less well defined than usual, and has no strong colouring. Strong noses and red hair do not come from a Cancerian Ascendant.

The Cancerian approach to things is highly personal. All general criticisms are taken personally, and all problems in any procedure for which they have responsibility is seen as a personal failing. As an Aquarian with a Cancerian way of working, you will be concerned to use your energies for the safe and secure establishment of things from the foundations up, so that you know that whatever you have been involved in has been done properly, and is unlikely to let you down in any way; you are concerned for your own safety and reputation. The other side of this approach is that you can be a little too concerned to make sure everything is done personally, and be unwilling to entrust things to other people. Not only does this overwork you, it seems obsessive and uncooperative to others.

The Cancer Ascendant person has health problems with the maintenance of the flow of fluids in his body, and a tendency to stomach ulcers caused by worry. Cancer Ascendant women should pay special attention to their breasts, since the affinity between the sign, the Moon as ruler of all things feminine, and that particular body system means that major imbalances in the life are likely to show there first. There could also be some problems with the liver and the circulation of the legs; the answer is to think that, metaphorically, you do not have to support everybody you know: they can use their own legs to stand on, and you do not have to feed them either.

## Leo Ascendant

You were born around sunset if you have Leo as an Ascendant. Leo as the determinant of the physical characteristics makes itself known by the lion of the sign—you can always spot the deep chest, proud and slightly pompous way of walking, and more often than not, the hair arranged in some sort of a mane, either full, taken back off the face, and golden if possible. Leo Ascendant people have strong voices and a definite presence to them. A Leo Ascendant will bring to the fore any hereditary tendency to golden colouring, so reddish or golden hair, or a rosy complexion may be in evidence, as will a heavy build in the upper half of the body.

The Leonine way of doing things is to put yourself in the centre and work from the centre outwards, making sure that everybody knows where the commands are coming from. It is quite a tiring way of working; you need to put a lot of energy into it, because you are acting as the driving force for everybody else. Preferred situations for this technique are those where you already know, more or less, what's going to happen; this way you are unlikely to be thrown off balance by unexpected developments. The grand gesture belongs to the Leo method; it works best if all process are converted into theatrical scenes, with roles acted rather than lived. Over-reaction, over-dramatization, and over-indulgence are common, but the approach is in essence kind-hearted and well-meant. Children enjoy being with Leo Ascendant people, and they enjoy having children around them. The flaws in the approach are only that little gets done in difficult circumstances where applause and appreciation are scarce commodities, and that little is attempted that is really new and innovatory.

The health problems of the Leo Ascendant person come from the heart, and also from the joints, which suffer from mobility problems. These both come from a lifetime of being at the centre of things and working for everybody's good, and from being too stiff and unwilling to try and change in position. The remedy, of course, is to be more flexible, and to allow your friends to repay the favours they owe you.

*Virgo Ascendant*
A birth in the early evening puts Virgo on the Ascendant. Physically, this should make you slim and rather long, especially in the body; even if you have broad shoulders you will still have a long

waist. There is a neatness to the features, but nothing notable; hair is brown, but again nothing notable. The nose and chin are often well-defined, and the forehead is often both tall and broad; the voice can be a little shrill and lacks penetration.

The Virgoan Ascendant person does not have an approach to life; he has a *system*. He analyses everything and pays a lot of attention to the way in which he works. It is important to the person with Virgo rising not only to be effective, but to be efficient; you can always interest them in a new or better technique. They watch themselves work, as if from a distance, all the while wondering if they can do it better. They never mind repetition; in fact they quite enjoy it, because as they get more proficient they feel better about things. To you, being able to do things is everything, and unless you are given a practical outlet for your energies, you are completely ineffective. There is a willingness to help others, to be of service through being able to offer a superior technique, inherent in the Virgo way of doing things, which prevents Virgo rising people from being seen as cold and unfriendly. The problems in the Virgo attitude are a tendency to go into things in more detail than is necessary, and to be too much concerned with the 'proper' way to do things.

People with a Virgo Ascendant are susceptible to intestinal problems and may be prone to circulatory problems, and poor sight. All of these are ways in which the body registers the stresses of being too concerned with digesting the minutiae of things which are meant to be passed through anyway, and by not getting enough social contact. The remedy is to lift your head from your workbench sometimes, admit that the act is sometimes more important than the manner of its performance, and not to take things too seriously.

## Libra Ascendant

You were born in the middle of the evening if you have Libra rising; it will give you a pleasant and approachable manner which will do a great deal to hide your anxieties and prevent people thinking anything but the best of you. You should be tallish, and graceful, as all Libra Ascendant people tend to be;

they have a clear complexion, and blue eyes if possible, set in an oval face with finely formed features.

The Libra Ascendant person has to go through life at a fairly relaxed pace. The sign that controls his body won't let him feel rushed or anxious; if that sort of thing looks likely, then he will slow down a little until the panic's over. There is a need to see yourself reflected in the eyes of others, and so you will form a large circle of friends. You define your own opinion of yourself through their responses to you, rather than being sure what you want, and not caring what they think.

The drawback to the Libran approach is that unless you have approval from others, you are unlikely to do anything on your own initiative, or at least you find it hard to decide on a course of action. You always want to do things in the way which will cause the least bother to anyone, and to produce an acceptable overall result; sometimes this isn't definite enough, and you need to know what you do want as well as what you don't.

The Libran Ascendant makes the body susceptible to all ailments of the kidneys and of the skin; there may also be trouble in the feet. The kidney ailments are from trying to take all the problems out of life as you go along. Sometimes it's better to simply attack a few of the obstacles and knock them flat in pure rage—and in doing so you will develop adrenaline from the adrenal glands, on top of the kidneys!

## Scorpio Ascendant

You were born towards midnight if you have a Scorpio Ascendant. A Scorpio Ascendant should give you a dark and powerful look with a solid build, though not necessarily over-muscled. Scorpio Ascendant people tend to have a very penetrating and level way of looking at others, which is often disconcerting. Any possible darkness in the colouring is usually displayed, with dark complexions and dark hair, often thick and curly, never fine.

The Scorpio Ascendant person usually does things in a controlled manner. He is not given to explosive releases of energy unless they are absolutely necessary; even then, not often. He knows, or feels (a better word, since the Scorpionic mind makes decisions as a result of knowledge gained by feeling rather than thinking), that he has plenty of energy to spare, but uses it in small and effective doses, each one suited to the requirements of the task at hand. It does not seem useful to him to put in more effort than is strictly necessary for any one activity; that extra energy could be used somewhere else. The idea that overdoing things for their own sakes is sometimes fun because of the sheer exhilaration of the release of energy does not strike a responsive chord in the Scorpio body, nor even much understanding. There is, however, understanding and perception of a situation which exists at more than one level. If anything is complicated, involving many activities and many people, with much interaction and many side issues which must be considered, then the Scorpio Ascendant person sees it all and understands all of it, in its minutest detail. They feel, and understand, the responses from all of their surroundings at once, but do not necessarily feel involved with them unless they choose to make a move. When they do move, they will have the intention of transforming things, making them different to conform to their ideas of how things need to be arranged.

Scorpio Ascendant people are unable simply to possess and look after anything; they must change it and direct it their way, and this can be a disadvantage.

Scorpio illnesses are usually to do with the genital and excretory systems; problems here relate to a lifestyle in which things are thrown away when used, or sometimes rejected when there is still use in them. It may be that there is too much stress on being the founder of the new, and on organizing others; this will bring head pains, and illnesses of that order. The solution is to take on the existing situation as it is, and look after it without changing any of it.

## Sagittarius Ascendant

It would have been in the small hours of the morning when you were born for you to have a Sagittarius Ascendant. If you have, you should be taller than average, with a sort of sporty, leggy look to you; you should have a long face with pronounced temples (you may be balding there if you are male), a well-coloured complexion, clear eyes, and brown hair. A Grecian nose is sometimes a feature of this physique.

The Sagittarian Ascendant gives a way of working that is based on mobility and change. This particular frame can't keep still and is much more comfortable walking than standing, more comfortable lounging or leaning than sitting formally. You tend to be in a bit of a hurry; travelling takes up a lot of your time, because you enjoy it so. It is probably true to say that you enjoy the process of driving more than whatever it is that you have to do when you get there. You probably think a lot of your car, and you are likely to have one which is more than just a machine for transport—you see it as an extension, a representation even, of yourself. People will notice how outgoing and friendly you seem to be, but they will need to know you for some time before they realize that you enjoy meeting people than almost anything else, and you dislike being with the same companions all the time. There is a constant restlessness in you; you will feel that being static is somehow unnatural, and it worries you. You are an optimist, but can also be an opportunist, in that you see no reason to stay doing one thing for a moment longer than it interests you. The inability to stay and develop a situation or give long-term commitment to anything is the biggest failing of this sign's influence.

A person with Sagittarius rising can expect to have problems with his hips and thighs, and possibly in his arterial system; this is to do with trying to leap too far at once, in all senses. You may also have liver and digestive problems, again caused by haste on a long-term scale. The remedy is to shorten your horizons and concentrate on things nearer home.

### Capricorn Ascendant

It must have been an hour or so before sunrise when you were born for you to have a Capricorn Ascendant. This sign often gives a small frame, quite compact and built to last a long time, the sort that doesn't need a lot of feeding and isn't big enough or heavy enough to break when it falls over. The face can be narrow and the features small; often the mouth points downwards at the corners, and this doesn't change even when the person smiles or laughs.

The Capricorn sees life as an ordered, dutiful struggle. There is a great deal of emphasis placed on projecting and maintaining appearances, both in the professional and the personal life; the idea of 'good reputation' is one which everybody with Capricorn rising, whatever their sun sign, recognizes at once. There is a sense of duty and commitment which the Sagittarian Ascendant simply cannot understand; here the feeling is that there are things which need doing, so you just have to set to and get them done. Capricorn Ascendant people see far forwards in time, anticipating their responsibilities for years to come, even if their Sun sign does not normally function this way; in such cases they apply themselves to one problem at a time, but can envisage a succession of such problems, one after another, going on for years.

The disadvantages of this outlook are to do with its static nature. There is often a sense of caution that borders on the paranoid, and while this is often well disguised in affluent middle-class middle age, it seems a little odd in the young. This tends to make for a critical assessment of all aspects of a new venture before embarking on it, and as a result a lot of the original impetus is lost. This makes the result less than was originally hoped in many cases, and so a cycle of disappointment and unadventurousness sets in, which is difficult to break. The Capricorn Ascendant person is often humourless, and can seem determined to remain so.

These people have trouble in their joints, and break bones from time to time, entirely as a result of being inflexible. On a small scale this can be from landing badly in an accident because the Capricorn Ascendant keeps up appearances to the very end, refusing to believe that an accident could be happening to him: on a large scale, a refusal to move with the times can lead to the collapse of an outmoded set of values when they are swept away by progress, and this breaking up of an old structure can also cripple. They can get lung troubles, too, as a result of not taking enough fresh air, or fresh ideas. The best treatment is to look after their families rather than their reputation, and to think about the difference between stability and stagnation.

## Aquarius Ascendant

Having an Aquarius Ascendant means that you were born around sunrise. This will make you more sociable than you would otherwise have been, with a strong interest in verbal communication. There is a certain clarity, not to say transparency, about the Aquarian physique. It is usually tall, fair, and well shaped, almost never small or dark. There is nothing about the face which is particularly distinctive; no noticeable colouring, shape of nose, brows, or any other feature. It is an average sort of face, cleanly formed and clear.

The person with an Aquarian Ascendant wants to be independent. Not violently so, not the sort of independence tht fights its way out of wherever it feels it's been put, just different from everybody else. Aquarius gives your body the ability to do things in ways perhaps not done before; you can discover new techniques and practices for yourself, and don't need to stay in the ways you were taught. There is a willingness to branch out, to try new things; not a Scorpionic wish to make things happen the way you want, but an amused curiosity which would just like to see if things are any better done a different way. There is no need for you to convince the world that your way is best: it only needs to suit you.

Of course, an Aquarian needs to measure his difference against others, and therefore you feel better when you have a few friends around you to bounce ideas off, as well as showing them how you're doing things in a slightly different way. You function best in groups, and feel physically at ease when you're not the only person in the room. You are not necessarily the leader of the group; just a group member. Group leaders put their energy into the group, and you draw strength and support from it, so you are unlikely to be the leader, though paradoxically all groups work better for having you in them.

A handicap arising from an Aquarian Ascendant is that you

are unlikely to really feel passionately involved with anything, and this may mean that unless you have support from your friends and colleagues you will be unable to muster the determination necessary to overcome really sizeable obstacles in your chosen career.

You are likely to suffer from diseases of the circulation and in your lower legs and ankles; these may reflect a life where too much time is spent trying to be independent, and not enough support is sought from others. You may also get stomach disorders and colds because you are not generating enough heat: get angrier and more involved in things!

## Pisces Ascendant

You were born in the middle of the morning if you have Pisces rising. Like Aries rising Pisces is only possible as an Ascendant for about fifty minutes, so there aren't many of you around.

Pisces Ascendant people are on the small side, with a tendency to be a bit pale and fleshy. They are not very well co-ordinated and so walk rather clumsily, despite the fact that their feet are often large. They have large, expressive, but rather sleepy-looking eyes.

As an Aquarian with Pisces rising, you will prefer to let things come to you rather than go out and look for them; and even more than the other Aquarians, you will need to be alone from time to time. The company of other people stimulates and inspires you, but you find yourself overwhelmed by the sheer volume of their ideas, and you need time to assess them. Your own opinions, the things you really believe in, will be very important to you— perhaps too important to show in public. Because you are so particularly sensitive to people's anxieties, you may find yourself wanting to do something positive to help, and could well become involved in some sort of research or charity work.

The major problem with a Pisces Asendant is the inability to be active rather than reactive; you would rather be reacting to outside influences than generating your own movements from within yourself.

A Piscean Ascendant gives problems with the feet and the

lymphatic system; this has connections with the way you move in response to external pressures, and how you deal with things which invade your system from outside. You may also suffer from faint-heartedness—literally as well as metaphorically. The remedy is to be more definite and less influenced by opinions other than your own.

# 6. Three Crosses: Areas of Life that Affect Each Other

If you have already determined your Ascendant sign from page 74, and you have read 'The Meaning Of The Zodiac' on page 11, you can apply that knowledge to every area of your life with revealing results. Instead of just looking at yourself, you can see how things like your career and your finances work from the unique point of view of your birth moment.

You will remember how the Ascendant defined which way up the sky was. Once you have it the right way up, then you can divide it into sectors for different areas of life, and see which zodiac signs occupy them. After that, you can interpret each sector of sky in the light of what you know about the zodiac sign which fell in it at the time that you were born.

Below there is a circular diagram of the sky, with horizon splitting it across the middle. This is the way real horoscopes are usually drawn. In the outer circle, in the space indicated, write the name of your Ascendant sign, not your Sun sign (unless they are the same, of course. If you don't know your time of birth, and so can't work out an Ascendant, use your Sun sign). Make it overlap sectors 12 and 1, so that the degree of your Ascendant within that sign is on the eastern horizon. Now fill in the rest of the zodiac around the circle in sequence, one across each sector boundary. If you've forgotten the sequence, look at the diagram on page 16. When you've done that, draw a symbol for the Sun ⊙—a circle with a point at its centre) in one of the sectors which has your Sun sign at its edge. Think about how far through the sign your Sun is; make sure that you have put it in the right sector. Whichever sector this is will be very important to you; having the sun there gives a bias to the whole chart, like the weight on one side of a locomotive wheel. You will feel that the activities of that sector (or house, as they are usually called) are most in keeping with your character, and you feel comfortable doing that sort of thing.

Make sure you have got your sums right. As an Aquarian born in the afternoon, you might well have Cancer rising, and the Sun in the 8th house, for example.

Now is the time to examine the twelve numbered sections of your own sky, and see what there is to be found.

## Angular Houses: 1, 4, 7, 10

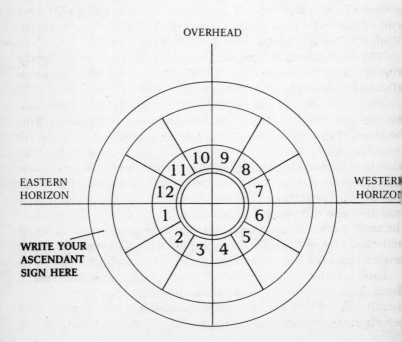

OVERHEAD

EASTERN
HORIZON

WESTERN
HORIZON

**WRITE YOUR
ASCENDANT
SIGN HERE**

These are the houses closest to the horizon and the vertical, reading round in zodiacal sequence. The first house is concerned with you yourself as a physical entity, your appearance, and your health. Most of this has been dealt with in the section on Ascendants. If you have the Sun here, it simply doubles the impact of your Sun sign energies.

Opposite to you is the seventh house, which concerns itself with everybody who is not you. Partners in a business sense, husbands, wives, enemies you are actually aware of (and who therefore stand opposed to you in plain sight) and any other unclassified strangers all belong in the seventh house. You see their motivation as being something you are not. If you have Capricorn rising, you see them as behaving, and needing to be treated, which is perhaps more accurate, in a Cancerian manner. This is how you approach seventh-house things. Use the keywords from 'The Meaning of the Zodiac' (p. 17) to remind yourself what this is. If you have the Sun in the seventh house you are your own best partner: you may marry late in life, or not at all. Perhaps your marriage will be unsuccessful. It is not a failure; it is simply that you are to a very great extent self-supporting, and have neither the ability nor the need to share yourself completely with another.

The whole business of the first and the seventh is to do with 'me and not-me'. For the personal energies of this relationship to be shown in tangible form, it is necessary to look at the pair of houses whose axis most squarely crosses the first/seventh axis. This is the fourth/tenth. The tenth is your received status in the world, and is the actual answer to the question 'What do you take me for?' No matter what you do, the world will find it best to see you as doing the sort of thing shown by the sign at the start of the tenth house. Eventually, you will start to pursue that kind of activity anyway, because in doing so you get more appreciation and reward from the rest of society.

Your efforts in dealing with others, which is a first/seven thing, have their result in the tenth, and their origins in the fourth. Expect to find clues there to your family, your home, the beliefs you hold most dear, and the eventual conclusion to your life (not your death, which is a different matter). If you have the Sun in the tenth, you will achieve some measure of prominence or fame; if your Sun is in the fourth, you will do well in property, and your family will be of greater importance to you than is usual.

There is, of course, some give and take between the paired houses. Giving more time to yourself in the first house means tht you are denying attention to the seventh, your partner; the reverse also applies. Giving a lot of attention to your career, in the tenth house, stops you from spending quite so much time as you might like with your family or at home. Spending too much time at home means that you are out of the public eye. There is only so much time in a day; what you give to one must be denied to the other.

This cross of four houses defines most people's life: self partner, home and career. An over-emphasis on any of these is to the detriment of the other three, and all the arms of the cross fee and react to any event affecting any single member.

If these four houses have cardinal signs on them in you chart, then you are very much the sort of person who feels tha he is in control of his own life, and that it is his duty to shape i into something new, personal, and original. You feel that b making decisive moves with your own circumstances you ca actually change the way your life unfolds, and enjoy steering i the way you want it to go.

If these four houses have fixed signs on them in your chart then you are the sort of person who sees the essential shape o our life as being one of looking after what you were given continuing in the tradition, and ending up with a profit at th end of it all. Like a farmer, you see yourself as a tenant of th land you inherited, with a responsibility to hand it on in at leas as good a condition as it was when you took it over. You are likel to see the main goal in all life's ups and downs as th maintenance of stability and enrichment of what you posses:

If these four houses have mutable signs on them in you chart, then you are much more willing to change yourself to su circumstances than the other two. Rather than seeing yourself a the captain of your ship, or the trustee of the family firm, you see yourself as free to adapt to challenges as they arise, and if necessary to make fundamental changes in your life, home and career to suit the needs of the moment. You are the sort to welcome change and novelty, and you don't expect to have anything to show for it at the end of the day except experience. There is a strong sense of service in the mutable signs, and if you spend your life working for the welfare of others, then they will have something to show for it while you will not. Not in physical terms, anyway; you will have had your reward by seeing your own energies transformed into their success.

## The Succedent Houses: 2, 5, 8, 11

These houses are called succedent because they succeed, or follow on from, the previous four. Where the angular houses define the framework of the life, the succedent ones give substance, and help develop it to its fullest and riches extent, in exactly the same way as fixed signs show the development and maintenance of the elemental energies defined by the cardinal signs.

The second house and the eighth define your resources; how much you have to play with, so to speak. The fifth and eleventh show what you do with it, and how much you achieve. Your immediate environment is the business of the second house. Your tastes in furniture and clothes are here (all part of your immediate environment, if you think about it) as well as your immediate resources, food and cash. Food is a resource because without it you are short of energy, and cash is a resource for obvious reasons. If you have the Sun here you are likely to be fond of spending money, and fond of eating too! You are likely to place value on things that you can buy or possess, and judge your success by your bank balance.

Opposed to it, and therefore dealing with the opposite viewpoint, is the eighth house, where you will find stored money. Savings, bank accounts, mortgages, and all kinds of non-immediate money come under this house. So do major and irreversible changes in your life, because they are the larger environment rather than the immediate one. Surgical operations and death are both in the eighth, because you are not the same person afterwards, and that is an irreversible change. If you have the Sun in the eighth you are likely to be very careful with yourself, and not the sort to expose yourself to any risk; you are also not likely to be short of a few thousand when life gets tight, because eighth house people always have some extra resource tucked away somewhere. You are also likely to benefit from legacies, which are another form of long-term wealth.

To turn all this money into some form of visible wealth you must obviously do something with it, and all forms of self-expression and ambition are found in the fifth and the eleventh houses. The fifth is where you have fun, basically; all that you like to do, all that amuses you, all your hobbies are found there, and a look at the zodiac sign falling in that house in your chart will show you what it is that you like so much. Your children are a fifth-house phenomenon, too; they are an expression of yourself made physical, made from the substance of your body and existence, and given their own. If you have the Sun in the fifth house you are likely to be of a generally happy disposition, confident that life is there to be enjoyed, and sure that something good will turn up.

The eleventh house, in contrast, is not so much what you like doing as what you would like to be doing: it deals with hopes, wishes, and ambitions. It also deals with friends and all social gatherings, because in a similar manner to the Aries/Libra axis, anybody who is 'not-you' and enjoying themselves must be opposed to you enjoying yourself in the fifth house. If you have the Sun in the eleventh house, you are at your best in a group. You would do well in large organizations, possibly political ones, and will find that you can organize well. You have well-defined ambitions, and know how to realize them, using other people as supporters of your cause.

The oppositions in this cross work just as effectively as the previous set did: cash is either used or stored, and to convert it from one to the other diminishes the first. Similarly, time spent enjoying yourself does nothing for your ambitions and aims, nor does it help you maintain relationships with all the groups of people you know; there again, all work and no play . . .

If you have Cardinal signs on these four houses in your chart, then you think that using all the resources available to you at any one time is important. Although what you do isn't necessarily important, or even stable, you want to have something to show for it, and enjoying yourself as you go along is important to you. To you, money is for spending, and how your friends see you is possibly more important to you than how you see yourself.

Fixed signs on these four houses will make you reticent, and careful of how you express yourself. You are possibly too busy with the important things of life as you see them, such as your career and long-term prospects, to give much attention to the way you live. You feel it is important to have things of quality, because you have a long-term view of life, and you feel secure when you have some money in the bank, but you don't enjoy your possessions and friends for your own sake. You have them because you feel that you should, not because they are reason enough in themselves.

Mutable signs on these four houses show a flexible attitude to the use of a resource, possibly because the angular houses show that you already have plenty of it, and it is your duty to use it well. You don't mind spending time and money on projects which to you are necessary, and which will have a measurable end result. You see that you need to spend time and effort to bring projects into a completed reality, and you are willing to do that as long as the final product is yours and worth having. You are likely to change your style of living quite frequently during your life, and there may be ambitions which, when fulfilled, fade from life completely.

## The Cadent Houses: 3, 6, 9, 12

The final four houses are called cadent either because they fall away from the angles (horizon and vertical axes), or because they fall towards them, giving their energy towards the formation of

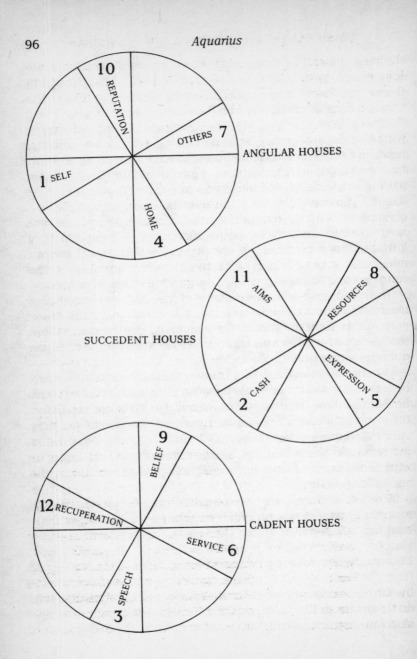

ANGULAR HOUSES

SUCCEDENT HOUSES

CADENT HOUSES

the next phase in their existence. Either way, affairs in these houses are nothing like as firm and active as those in the other two sets of four. It may be useful to think of them as being given to mental rather than physical or material activities.

The third and ninth houses are given to thought and speech, with the ninth specializing in incoming thoughts, such as reading, learning and belief (religions of all kinds are ninth-house things), while the third limits itself to speaking and writing, daily chat, and the sort of conversations you have every day. If you have the sun in the third house, you will be a chatterbox. Talking is something you could do all day, and you love reading. Anything will do—papers, magazines, novels; as long as it has words in it you will like it. You will have the sort of mind that loves accumulating trivia, but you may find that serious study or hard learning is something that you cannot do.

The third house concerns itself with daily conversation, but the ninth is more withdrawn. Study is easy for a ninth-house person, but since all ideal and theoretical thought belongs here, the down-to-earth street-corner reality of the third house doesn't, and so the higher knowledge of the ninth finds no application in daily life. The third-ninth axis is the difference between practical street experience and the refined learning of a university. To give time to one must mean taking time from the other. If you have the Sun in the ninth, you are likely to hve a very sure grasp of the theory of things, and could well be an instigator or director of large projects; but you are unable to actually do the things yourself. Knowledge is yours, but application is not.

How this knowledge gets applied in the production of something new is a matter of technique, and technique is the business of the sixth house. The way things get done, both for yourself and for other people's benefit, is all in the sixth. Everything you do on someone else's behalf is there, too. If you have the Sun in the sixth house, you are careful and considerate by nature, much concerned to make the best use of things and to do things in the best way possible. Pride of work and craftsman-ship are guiding words to you; any kind of sloppiness is upsetting. You look after yourself, too; health is a sixth-house thing, and the Sun in the sixth sometimes makes you something of a hypochondriac.

Opposed to the sixth, and therefore opposed to the ideas of doing things for others, mastering the proper technique, and looking after your physical health, is the twelfth house. This is concerned with withdrawing yourself from the world, being on your own, having time to think. Energy is applied to the job in hand in the sixth house, and here it is allowed to grow again without being applied to anything. Recuperation is a good word to remember. All forms of rest are twelfth-house concepts. If you have the Sun in the twelfth house you are an essentially private individual, and there will be times when you need to be on your own to think about things and recover your strength and balance. You will keep your opinions to yourself, and share very little of your emotional troubles with anyone. Yours is most definitely not a life lived out in the open.

These houses live in the shadow of the houses which follow them. Each of them is a preparation for the next phase. If your Sun is in any of these houses, your life is much more one of giving away than of accumulation. You already have the experience and the knowledge, and you will be trying to hand it on before you go, so to speak. Acquisition is something you will never manage on a permanent basis.

If these houses have Cardinal signs on them in your chart, then preparation for things to come is important to you, and you think in straight lines towards a recognized goal. You will have firm and rather simplistic views and beliefs about matters which are not usually described in such terms, such as morality and politics, and you will be used to saying things simply and with meaning. Deception and half-truths, even mild exaggeration, confuse you, because you do not think in that sort of way.

If fixed signs occupy these houses in your horoscope, your thinking is conservative, and your mind, though rich and varied in its imagination, is not truly original. You like to collect ideas from elsewhere and tell yourself that they are your own. You rely on changing circumstances to bring you variety, and your own beliefs and opinions stay fixed to anchor you in a changing world; unfortunately, this can mean a refusal to take in new ideas, shown in your behaviour as a rather appealing old-fashionedness.

Having mutable signs on these houses in your horoscope shows a flexible imagination, though often not a very practical one. Speech and ideas flow freely from you, and you are quick to adapt your ideas to suit the occasion, performing complete changes of viewpoint without effort if required. You seem to have grasped the instinctive truth that mental images and words are not real, and can be changed or erased at will; you are far less inhibited in their use than the other two groups, who regard words as something at least as heavy as cement, and nearly as difficult to dissolve. Periods in the public eye and periods of isolation are of equal value to you; you can use them each for their best purpose, and have no dislike of either. This great flexibility of mind does mean, though, that you lack seriousness of approach at times, and have a happy-go-lucky view of the future, and of things spiritual, which may lead to eventual disappointments and regrets.

Houses are important in a horoscope. The twelve sectors of the sky correspond to the twelve signs of the zodiac, the difference being that the zodiac is a product of the Sun's annual revolution, and the houses are a product (via the Ascendant) of the Earth's daily revolution. They bring the symbolism down one level from the sky to the individual, and they answer the questions which arise when people of the same Sun sign have different lives and different preferences. The house in which the Sun falls, and the qualities of the signs in the houses, show each person's approach to those areas of his life, and the one which will be the most important to him.

Part 4

# Aquarius Trivia

# 7. Tastes and Preferences

## Clothes

Aquarians don't dress in the same way as Capricorns at all. There's no reason why they should, since they are a different sign, but the two signs are ruled by the same planet, so you might expect a few similarities. There are some, but they will only become apparent later; for the moment, have a look at the surface effect of Aquarian dressing. What really characterizes Aquarian dressing is the desire to look different from everybody else.

Dressing so that you stand out in the crowd does two things, both of which an Aquarian is keen to achieve. Firstly, it marks you as an individual, somebody who thinks, and probably acts, in a manner apart from everyone else. Secondly, it isolates you; nobody can feel that he is similar to you because his clothes don't say the same things as yours; in addition, if your clothes have a message which is new or unfamiliar to those who see it, then it says nothing about the individual inside. What you have managed to do by dressing unconventionally is to say that you are different, and that you are unknowable, at the same time. This is exactly what you are like, of course; you like to stay impersonal, slightly removed from the jostle of everybody else's emotional traffic.

Here is the similarity between Capricorn and Aquarius. The

principle is that of enclosure and separation, which seems reasonable when you remember that Saturn is behind it. Capricorn wears formal and expensive clothes, to set himself apart by his status and position; Aquarius wears unusual clothes, to separate himself from the crowd he is usually part of.

In your actual choice of clothes, you are very varied. Often you will choose something which shows your allegiance to a particular set of ideas, rather than anything about you personally. The result is something of a uniform, something that other people from your group can recognize. It may be the working clothes of your profession, or it may be the scarf and hat of your favourite football team. It may represent some identifiable political group, such as the natural earth tones favoured by most environmentalists, or the red tie which used to be so popular with Socialists.

Left to your own devices, you will probably choose things which come in neat, small shapes, without much fussy detailing. At the same time, you will be looking for something different in the cut or the decoration—something which will say 'the wearer of this garment is very different from what you think'. For this reason you are likely to go for asymmetric designs, or zigzag lines. Aquarians of both sexes like clothes with diagonal lines in the design, and also anything which is recognizably futuristic; there is a sort of impersonal, scientific look to most clothes like that which has a great deal of appeal to you.

You're not fussy about the feel of the fabric, unlike, say, the Taureans; you are far more likely to make a logical choice on the grounds of how easy it is to wash, how long it will last, and things like that. You have no objection to modern fabrics, or even plastics; in fact you rather like them, because there is an element of enclosure and insulation associated with them, as well as a certain coldness. The plastic mac must be an Aquarian garment, then, but so is the boiler suit, and so, to a certain extent, are jeans: they were originally workwear, they came to symbolize a set of values, they were truly universal, transcending all barriers of class and sex, and they are—at least when new—indigo blue, the colour of the sign.

## Food and Furnishings

Aquarians have universal taste in food; they will usually eat absolutely anything, as long as everybody else is having the same thing. The idea is to be part of the group, as usual. Sometimes their choice in food represents their current interest; if they are campaigning to save the world's resources and to ban the use of chemical additives, they will change their diet to consist of organic wholefoods. Like the other Saturnine sign, Capricorn, they don't overeat, and they are not usually interested in food as a source of pleasure; they eat because they are hungry.

An Aquarian's home is likely to reflect his emotional tone; it will be cool and airy, full of interesting things, but not cluttered. The colour blue may predominate, but not so that you would really notice. Air signs like to circulate, and they like the air to move in their houses; consequently they leave doors open as they wander from room to room, involved in lots of things at once. Aquarians have strangely retentive tastes, in that they find something that they like and then stay with it for a long time; furniture is a fairly long-lasting item in anyone's home, but you may find things in an Aquarian home that you thought everybody had thrown out years ago. Often there is something in chrome and glass, such as a table, or a futuristic light fitting; the combination of cool, hard and transparent appeals to the person from the Lunar side of Saturn in the zodiac.

## Hobbies

Aquarians are often too deeply immersed in what they are working at to take time off for pastimes. They tend to live their beliefs round the clock, especially if they have a political interest, or support some humanitarian cause. Those who do have time for other interests usually find something which gets them into their element, the air. Walking and climbing are popular, because the wind is usually noticeable, and so is driving an open-topped car. Hang-gliding and all forms of flying appeal for the same reason: you feel yourself moving in the air.

A lot of Aquarians have mechanical interests, such as fiddling with engines of one sort or another. This is a perfect combination of the hardness of Saturn and the logical thinking of Aquarius, and keeps them happy for hours. So does anything scientific, such as astronomy.

All Aquarians are great socializers, of course, and love going to parties: it's where their particular energy can be at its best. They are not, however, great sportsmen, probably because their interest in themselves is intellectual rather than physical. They might like badminton; you can see the effect of the air on the shuttlecock!

# 8. Aquarian Luck

Being lucky isn't a matter of pure luck. It can be engineered. What happens when you are lucky is that a number of correspondences are made between circumstances, people, and even material items, which eventually enable planetary energies to flow quickly and effectively to act with full force in a particular way. If you are part of that chain, or your intentions lie in the same direction as the planetary flow, then you say that things are going your way, or that you are lucky. All you have to do to maximize this tendency is to make sure you are aligned to the flow of energies from the planets whenever you want things to work our way.

It is regular astrological practice to try to reinforce your own position in these things, by attracting energies which are already strongly represented in you. For Aquarius, this means Saturn, of course, and therefore any 'lucky' number, colour, or whatever for an Aquarian is simply going to be one of those which correspond symbolically with the attributes of Saturn.

Saturn's colour is black, and the colours of Aquarius itself are various blues, sometimes indigo, and sometimes electric blue; and therefore an Aquarian's lucky colours are black and blue, because by wearing them or aligning himself to them, for example by betting on a horse whose jockey's silks are black and blue, or supporting a sporting team whose colours include black or blue, he aligns himself to the energies of Saturn and his sign, and thereby recharges the Solar energies that are already in him.

Aquarius' preferred gemstone is a sapphire; lapis lazuli is sometimes quoted too. Gemstones are seen as being able to concentrate or focus magical energies, and the colour of the stone shows its propensity to the energies of a particular planet. There are other stones quoted for the sign, such as chalcedony; in most cases it is the colour which is the key.

Because Aquarius is the eleventh sign, your lucky number is 11. Saturn has its own number, which is 4 (though some authorities quote 3); that will be lucky for you too, and all combinations of numbers which add up to 4 by reduction work the same way, so you have a range to choose from. Reducing a number is done by adding its digits until you can go no further. As an example, take 472, $4 + 7 + 2 = 13$, and then $1 + 3 = 4$. There you are—472 is a lucky number for you, so to buy a car with those digits in its registration plate would make it a car which, while you had it, you were very fond of, and which served you well.

Saturn also has its own day, Saturday (Saturn's Day, yes?), and Aquarius has a direction with which it is associated, the north-west. If you have something important to do, and you manage to put it into action on Saturday 4th November (month number 11, remember), then you will have made sure that you will get the result best suited to you by aligning yourself to your own planet and helping its energies flow through you and your activity unimpeded.

Saturn also has a metal associated with it, and in the Middle Ages people wore jewellery made of their planetary metals for luck, or self-alignment and emphasis, whichever way you want to describe it. In the case of Aquarius and Saturn, that metal is lead. I know you are not likely to wear jewellery made of lead, but those Aquarians who care for mankind and his environment might be interested in its capabilites as a shield against radiation. Since you represent the lunar side of Saturn, how about a silver ring (silver is the Moon's metal) set with a sapphire?

There are also plants for each planet, and foods too. Among

Saturn's plants are mandrake and deadly nightshade, the vegetables spinach and parsnip, and the herb, sage. There is almost no end to the list of correspondences between the planets and everyday items, and many more can be made if you have a good imagination. They are lucky for Aquarians if you know what makes them so, and if you believe them to be so; the essence of the process lies in linking yourself and the object of your intent with some identifiable token of your own planet, such as its colour or number, and strengthening yourself thereby. The stronger you are, then the more frequently you will be able to achieve the result you want—and that's all that luck is, isn't it?

# A Final Word

By the time you reach here, you will have learnt a great deal more about yourself. At least, I hope you have.

You will probably have noticed that I appear to have contradicted myself in some parts of the book, and have repeated myself in others, and there are reasons for this. It is quite likely that I have said that your Sun position makes you one way, while your Ascendant makes you the opposite. There is nothing strange about this; nobody is consistent, the same the whole way through—everybody has contradictory sides to their character, and knowing some more about your Sun sign and your Ascendant will help you to label and define those contradictory elements. It won't do anything about dealing with them, though—that's your job, and always has been. The only person who can live your horoscope is you. Astrology won't make your problems disappear, and it never has been able to; it simply defines the problems more clearly, and enables you to look for answers.

Where I have repeated myself it is either to make the point for the benefit of the person who is only going to read that section of the book, or because you have a double helping of the energy of your sign, as in the instance of the Sun and Ascendant in the same sign.

I hope you found the relationships section useful; you may well find that the Sun-to-Ascendant comparison is just as useful in showing you how you fit in with your partner as the usual Sun-to-Sun practice.

Where do you go from here? If you want to learn more about astrology, and see how all of the planets fit into the picture of the sky as it was at your birth, then you must either consult an astrologer or learn how to do it for yourself. There is quite a lot of astrology around these days; evening classes are not too hard to find and there are groups of enthusiasts up and down the country. There are also plenty of books which will show you how to draw up and interpret your own horoscope.

One thing about doing it yourself, which is an annoyance unless you are aware of it in advance: to calculate your horoscope properly you will need to know where the planets were in the sky when you were born, and you usually have to buy this data separately in a book called an ephemeris. The reason that astrology books don't have this data in them is that to include enough for everybody who is likely to buy the book would make the book as big as a 'phone directory, and look like a giant book of log tables, which is a bit off-putting. You can buy ephemerides (the plural) for any single year, such as the one of your birth. You can also buy omnibus versions for the whole century.

So, you will need two books, not one: an ephemeris, and a book to help you draw up and interpret your horoscope. It's much less annoying when you *know* you're going to need two books.

After that, there are lots of books on the more advanced techniques in the Astrology Handbook series, also from the Aquarian Press. Good though the books are, there is no substitute for being taught by an astrologer, and no substitute at all for practice. What we are trying to do here is provide a vocabulary of symbols taken from the sky so that you and your imagination can make sense of the world you live in; the essential element is your imagination, and you provide that.

Astrology works perfectly well at Sun sign level, and it works perfectly well at deeper levels as well; you can do it with what you want. I hope that, whatever you do with it, it is both instructive and satisfying to you—and fun, too.

# SUNS AND LOVERS

## The Astrology of Sexual Relationships

**Penny Thornton**. It doesn't seem to matter how experienced – or inexperienced – you are, when it comes to love and romance there just *isn't* a fool proof formula. . . but this book does its best to provide one! THE definitive astrological guide to sexual relationships, this book is based upon the accumulated wisdom, and observations of centuries of dedicated astrologists. Reveals:

- In-depth analysis of astrological types
- Male and female profiles for each star sign
- Zodiacal attitudes to intimate relationships
- Most compatible – and incompatible – partners

Each general star sign analysis is concluded with amazingly frank reflections, often based upon personal interviews, with many famous personalities including: Bob Champion; Suzi Quatro; Colin Wilson; Jeremy Irons; HRH The Princess Anne; HRH The Duke of York; Martin Shaw; Barbara Cartland; Twiggy and many more. Written in an easy-to-read style, and packed with illuminating and fascinating tit-bits, this book is compulsive reading for anyone likely to have *any sort* of encounter with the opposite sex!